SHOW ME THE EVIDENCE

MIRACULOUS DISPLAYS OF GOD'S POWER IN CRITICAL TIMES

VALENTINE A. RODNEY

For Conferences, Workshop, Crusades, Conventions and Seminars contact:

Rev. Valentine Rodney
c/o Word Impact Ministries International
P.O. Box 787
Spanish Town
St. Catherine
Jamaica

Email: varodney@gmail.com

Tel: Jamaica: 876 390 2303 | USA: 407 545 5052

Published by:

ISBN: 978-1-958404-99-7 (paperback)
978-1-965635-00-1 (hardback)

First Edition: August 2024

This work is dedicated to all believers who have been patiently waiting for the unfolding of God's purpose in their lives.

To those who have been through the crucible of hardships and the furnace affliction, may your trust and hope be in King Jesus, our Lord. May the question concerning why God permits suffering in the life of a believer be revealed to His honour and glory.

ACKNOWLEDGEMENT

I owe a debt of gratitude to my Lord and Saviour Jesus Christ by whose grace, sovereignty and all-sufficiency I stand. Without Him, my journey would have ended abruptly. He indeed is the resurrection and the life.

To Pastor Sophia Martin from Empowered To Win Ministry, Canada that not only facilitated my ministry trip to Canada but provided compassionate and unwavering support during my health ordeal. I call her my sister who assumed the role of mothering.

What can I say about my wife, Yevett Thomas-Rodney, who stood by me and provided such invaluable moral and emotional support. She was there with me in the ICU most days from morning until night. Her presence made the hospitalisation a bit more bearable as I would so look forward to her arrival to lift my spirit and provide both cheer and hope. Not only was she there during the hospitalisation but stayed with me an entire month after discharge to attend to me personally, and we made the trip together back to Jamaica. I certainly married good.

To my sister who flew from Jamaica with my wife making me a priority as you rearranged all your plans. Your questions were vital to the healthcare workers who responded with alacrity and made things so much easier. You are worth your weight in gold (no pun intended).

There are so many others from the churched and unchurched community that sent their prayers and goodwill wishes that indeed played a role in my rapid recovery.

The Empowered to Win family led by Pastor Sophia Martin stood their ground as they declared "You will not die but live to declare the works of the Lord. Amen." I appreciate the calls, text messages, hospital visits, home visits and just the general love and support from the Christian community. They prayed in their homes, at church, special meetings and online from so many countries too numerous to mention.

They had a firm and unwavering belief that God was not through with me yet, so they persevered in prayer. They demonstrated a level of audacity in prayer, believing that it was God's will for my condition to change for the better with nothing missing and nothing lacking. "All the faculties that were needed to continue ministry would be restored," they believed and reiterated every chance they got.

FOREWORD

We live in a very interesting age where there is some measure of confusion about the nature and relevance of the church in our day. Having plummeted through a global pandemic that took many lives, with the only "cure' being to get vaccinated, there was much confusion in the church that provoked many to ask, 'Where is the evidence of our faith?"

Sometimes it is easy to talk about faith when we are observing what others are going through from the outside. The reality of a heavenly protocol seldom hits home until calamity approaches our own doorsteps. We know the church has been praying for over 2000 years "on earth as it is in heaven," but the full manifestation of that reality is yet to be realized as many believers grapple with the idea that faith can produce an alternate reality to what we may be experiencing on earth. Jesus encountered many who could not hear, speak, see or walk, and He manifested a contrasting reality that could have only come from a heavenly dimension. The physical world is not the only world there is. Even those Jesus encountered who were dead received something quite unexpected: another chance. We need to understand the spiritual technology at work here. We know when the soul/spirit of a person departs, the body dies. To which world does the soul/spirit go? Jesus apparently has pre-eminence in all worlds—in all existing realities—that He can call that soul/spirit from another world to return to the body in this world that we know. Didn't He say we also have that authority?

If faith is the substance and the evidence, it means it must be seen and experienced. Faith is not just an idea, a fleeting concept, or a hot topic for a charismatic message, but a living reality that can shift a soul from damnation to redemption. It has the potent power to give life where there is death, and to dramatically change lives.

Bishop Valantine Rodney was carrying out his divine mission as usual when the unexpected occurred. His living reality changed in almost a moment to something quite the opposite. He was pulled quite reluctantly into the clutching jaws of trauma and taken to the threshold between life and death. This is the road that many have walked, and only some have returned from, save the divine intervention of God.

It is often said that there is no testimony without a test, and many believers live off the glory of other's testimony, unable apparently to find their own. For this man of God who preaches and teaches faith, the mettle of his own capacity and those connected to him to walk out what he preaches was tested. With the immediacy that darkness can come upon us, equally there was an immediacy in response from the faith community and divine intervention that pulled the man of God from the brink of transition, allowing him to experience full access to the resurrection power that has been gifted to the body of Christ. A living, breathing life is a true testament to the power of God to redeem and retore, and I believe this book and its added theological reflections will challenge our own faith to believe for greater, not just for our selves and immediate family, but the nations to whom we are called to share the glorious gospel with.

Cleveland Orville McLeish
Author and Senior Copy Editor
Book Publisher
www.clevelandomcleish.com

ABOUT THE AUTHOR

REV. VALENTINE A. RODNEY, BSc, MA. is an international speaker whose ministry has taken him to the USA, Canada, Europe, Africa, and several countries within the Caribbean, where he has also fostered and facilitated ministerial developmental programmes. He has done undergraduate work at the University of the West Indies in Marine Biology and Graduate work in Missions at the Caribbean Graduate School of Theology. Rev. Rodney has served in the areas of Christian Education, Evangelism, Leadership Development, Prayer and Intercession, Youth Ministry, Radio and Television and Pastorate. He is also actively involved in welfare programmes and mentorship to men, youths, and ministers. He is a strong advocate for Christian Transformational Development where the church interfaces with the community and assists in strategic intervention that is both redemptive and empowering.

He is the author of the books, Shameless Persistence: The Audacity Of Purposeful Praying, A Way of Escape: How To Handle The Tests And Temptations Of Life, The Power of the Secret Place: The Place Of Relationship, Resolution And Revelation, and several other amazon bestsellers. Rev. Rodney assisted in the establishment and development of several bible schools and has lectured part time at the Jamaica Theological Seminary. He is the host and presenter of the television programme Word Impact aired on the cable station Mercy and Truth TV.

Rev. Rodney is an International Instructor for Walk Thru The Bible Ministries, Director of Word Impact Seminar Events and Word Impact Ministries International, a non-denominational ministry that caters to the empowerment of the Christian Community and the salvation of the lost. He is an International Chaplain and Ambassador with Covenant International University and Seminary. His Motto is *"Go Where There Is No Path and Leave a Trail."*

VALENTINE A. RODNEY is married to Yevett for over twenty-eight years. Their union has produced two daughters, Zharia and Ana-Olivia.

TABLE OF CONTENTS

CHAPTER 1

THE JOURNEY

Sometimes the journey of life can have so many unpredictable twists and turns. However, we are guided by the fact that the omniscient and omnipresent God is both aware and has been where we are yet to reach. Misfortune does not signal the absence of God or a lack/loss of His providential care. A closed door is never a lost cause. Some delays are divine in origin and must be embraced as such. Not everything can and must be done in haste. There are things that require patient continuance. That quality of endurance is tied to hope. It will be, but we, with patience, will wait for it.

The narrative of Joseph in the Old Testament makes it abundantly clear that God can be with you despite experiencing a series of misfortunes. Never judge the season of your life by the adversities you face. A downward spiral does not mean the end of the road or the death of dreams. As we build resilience through the crucible of hardships, we are confident that we are not forsaken or forgotten and that, in due time, we shall experience the goodness of God in the land of the living.

In December 2023, I bravely announced that the year 2024 would be a time of restoration. Note keenly that there can be no restoration unless one has incurred losses. In the act of restoration, God ensures that the believer is in a far better position than just receiving what was lost. Accumulated benefits will accrue commensurate with the losses that have been experienced prior to and within the year. We would do well to be reassured and encouraged by these words "We cannot now His purpose see but tis God's hands that leadeth me."

I was completely excited about the time of ministry in Canada and looked forward to empowering and edifying the people of God. I completed my first assignment with Pastor Sophia Martin of Empowered to Win Ministries Canada for their Easter Revival from March 29th to 31st. During that weekend of ministry, there were salvation experiences for several men and the delivering of souls from varying levels of challenges and distress. Prayer was offered for stubborn, unresolved situations from which testimonies have already been received with a positive outcome, all to the glory of God and the exaltation of His name.

Nothing could have prepared me adequately for the storms and whirlwind that was headed in my direction. In retrospect, I take great comfort in the words of the scriptures concerning the approach to adversity.

Dear friends, don't be surprised at the fiery trials you are going through, as if something strange were happening to you. Instead, be very glad—for these trials make you partners with Christ in his suffering, so that you will have the wonderful joy of seeing his glory when it is revealed to all the world. If you are insulted because you bear the name of Christ, you will be blessed, for the glorious Spirit of God rests upon you. If you suffer, however, it must not be for murder, stealing, making trouble, or prying into other people's affairs. But it is no shame to suffer for being a Christian. Praise God for the privilege of being called by his name! (1 Peter 4: 12-16 - NLT).

The most profound revelation is the understanding that God prepares you for the inevitable and never leaves you during the process. I was also to learn the invaluable lesson of trial and faith.

Dear brothers and sisters, when troubles of any kind come your way, consider it an opportunity for great joy. For you know that when your faith is tested, your endurance has a chance to grow. So let it grow, for when your endurance is fully developed, you will be perfect and complete, needing nothing. (James 1:2-4 - NLT).

During the days and weeks ahead, I was going to learn that God's peace that comes via the Holy Spirit can sustain in any adversarial season. But most importantly, how the Christian community can rally to a cause to support when you are at the lowest level of your life.

VERTIGO AND HEADACHES

I was on a break between assignments when, on the 3rd of April, in the evening, I began to have an extreme case of vertigo. It seemed as if the entire room was spinning, and I had extreme difficulty walking or even standing up. It brought with it nausea and an overwhelming sense of weakness. Coupled with that was a searing headache, the likes of which I had never felt before, especially when I coughed.

Elder Stanberry, the head of the family that hosted me, inquired if I was well or if I desired to be taken to the doctor. I quickly consented to the visit, not liking how I felt. I remember praying and saying, "God, not here and certainly not now." I trusted that this would be temporary and perhaps, with some rest, would pass.

I went to the bathroom to shower in anticipation of being taken for a checkup. Because of my instability, I ended up pulling down the racks, and everything was on the ground. I could not bend over for fear of falling, which I did a few times. I quickly made my way to the bedroom, hoping to sleep it off, but that never happened immediately. Everything in the room kept spinning, and even the bed felt unsteady. I kept reminding myself that I would not be afraid but continue to ride out the feelings that came in waves. In my heart, I just had the conviction that this would never be how my story ends. After all, I had a ministry engagement beginning the weekend with Pastor Richard, which I needed to attend. Pastor Martin was called and came by to check up on me. She, along with members of the household, had me under observation, trusting that this bout of sickness would break.

Things only further declined on Thursday, and it was difficult for me to perform simple functions without the offer of assistance, which I kept turning down. I was left at home with Elder Stanberry and Sister Awrita. I started to vomit, and my blood pressure skyrocketed. Then started the onset of more severe headaches. By then, I had stopped eating and kept drinking tea. I started displaying what I thought were flu-like symptoms with the usual postnasal drip and frequent coughs and chills. No over-the-counter medication that I took seemed to stem the coughing and flow of mucous.

My ability to balance was severely compromised, and I was very unsteady in my gait. In the morning (Friday), I was assisted in coming downstairs by Sis. Corrona and Pastor Martin. I was very unsteady in my legs, and even my grip was very weak. I was told that I gleefully shouted out that I felt like a baby. I was taken to the doctor, who gave me some hydration fluids. The doctor assessed that I had influenza B and questioned where I had been prior to coming to Canada to see if I had been exposed to some other virus. I was given a plethora of medication including probiotics, painkillers, and hydration fluids.

Sis. Sophia asked me to squeeze her hand; the left was okay, but the right was not. Unable to walk. Damone Evans assisted in taking me to the doctor. I was asked a few questions, but my answers were vague. The symptoms, they said, mirrored bird flu. They prescribed antibiotics, Pedialyte, and Tylenol for headaches. I was unable to walk from the car to the house. I was ably assisted by three individuals into the house, tucked in downstairs, and doors open to allow for fresh air.

Friday afternoon, I kept going to the washroom, repeatedly assisted by Elder Stanberry. Based on further deterioration in my state, I was immediately prepared and dressed for the hospital. He indicated that at that time, I had no power in my hand and was unable to stand and maintain my balance. I stumbled and fell a couple of times in the washroom and off the bed.

Elder indicated that I was unresponsive to any form of questioning and was reluctant to accept any offer of help. I was lifted onto Elder Stanberry's back and taken to the vehicle, where I was strapped in. Elder Cedrick Stanberry and Pastor Brown assisted me in preparation for the trip to the Brampton Hospital. I was unable to dress myself but was ably assisted by these two men.

BRAMPTON CIVIC HOSPITAL

After registration, I was admitted at about 3-4AM on Saturday morning. I did two MRIs to determine the cause of my illness. On admittance, blood work started, of which I was totally unaware. I had to be prompted to speak;

otherwise, I would remain quiet. I was responsive but not aware of my surroundings. The diagnosis after the MRI at the Brampton Hospital was that there was a blood clot at the back of the head. The diagnosis at that time was not clear whether it was a tumor or not. I was subsequently transferred to the Mississauga Hospital for further analysis and treatment.

The transfer from Brampton to Mississauga on Saturday night was executed based on the nature of the emergency. I was operated on the same night based on the blood and water seen on the brain. The doctors indicated that it was abnormal to have a stroke within that area of the brain where it was presented.

ISCHEMIC STROKE

I kept complaining about intense pain in my head. I was escorted in a wheelchair to be registered on arrival at the Brampton Civic Hospital. At that time, I was unable to answer the questions I was asked at registration. Tea and food were procured as I was very hungry. Pastor Sophia remarked that if this were a loyalty test in preparation for her husband, she would pass it in taking care of the man of God.

Whilst at the Brampton health facility, I was told that I had a telephone conversation with my wife, who was now cognizant of what had transpired. She asked me whether she should attend the Biannual Parish convention on Saturday, and I said yes. I was totally unaware at that time of the gravity of the situation. My sister at that time was visiting Jamaica so based on the reports received, both decided to come to Canada the very next day.

Miraculously, the finances came through for both my wife and sister to make the trip. My sister's husband, who was on the Island, took them to the Montego Bay (Jamaica) airport for the flight to Toronto (Canada).

Pastor Sophia Martin stayed with me after sending the Stanberrys home. I went into the emergency section and was admitted due to the high blood pressure readings. Two nurses and a doctor were assigned to me at that time. They recommended that both a CT scan and MRI be done. My blood pressure readings rose to 190/120 at one stage. No neurologist was on site, so the information was sent to Trillium Hospital in Mississauga for analysis. My eyes were closed most of the time, and I kept drifting in and out of consciousness. Two other scans were subsequently done, and the reports were sent to the Trillium Health Partners Hospital for analysis and recommendation. Pastor Martin was subsequently relieved by Pastor and Lady Richards on Saturday.

Around 11 pm, my sister was contacted and told to inform my wife. My wife was contacted by video call, and we spoke for about forty minutes while I was hospitalized at Brampton. At one point, I felt like I was being moved from one place to another, and I saw lighted glass cubicles with medical instructions and designs that were stationary, almost like a display.

THE SCARE

On Sunday morning, when Pastor Martin returned to the room that I was admitted to, it was vacant, with the bed neatly made up. She was frantic on hearing that I may have been discharged and fell to the ground screaming, despairing of hope. Further checks subsequently revealed that I was transferred to Trillium Health Partners Hospital in Mississauga. There was bleeding and fluids on the brain, and Brampton Hospital was not equipped to deal with this emergency. They also indicated that it was high risk and were unsure if I would make it. From admittance to now transferal, things had progressively declined, and they were unable to get me stabilized at Brampton, hence the transferal to a more specialized hospital.

TRILLIUM HEALTH PARTNERS HOSPITAL, MISSISSAUGA

Neurologists and Neurosurgeons indicated that the stroke was at the back of the head. They indicated that it had happened in a most unlikely area, and it was the first time they were witnessing that type of stroke in that area of the brain, even though it could and had happened. When they heard that I was a minister, they wanted to send for a chaplain to offer up religious service on my behalf, but this was declined as it carried an ominous air of finality. It was something akin to a last rite.

They determined that I was positive for Influenza B and I had developed an Ischemic stroke. I was attached to a breathing machine (ventilator) because I was unable to breathe by myself. For several hours, my condition was not improving. I was prescribed a different blood pressure medication as well as medication for influenza. They indicated that youth was in my favour and that it was possible I would pull through. I remember hearing one doctor remark that some young men less than twice my age did not recover from less severe strokes.

My thoughts of a brief stay progressively eroded based on the dawning serious situation. I realized that the completion of the rest of my assignments was no longer a possibility; thus, the focus must now be on getting better.

On Monday morning, I woke up to see on the charts that I had extubated myself. I had removed the breathing tube and was breathing on my own. The breathing tube was never reinserted as they realized it was no longer needed. By that time, my wife, Yevett, and my sister, June (Marie), had flown into Canada from Jamaica. I started talking after that and was very upbeat. Pastor Martin attributed my change in attitude to that of seeing and hearing my wife, to which I agreed.

CHAPTER 2

WHERE IS THE EVIDENCE?

During the forty days after he suffered and died, he appeared to the apostles from time to time, and he proved to them in many ways that he was actually alive. And he talked to them about the Kingdom of God. (Acts 1:3 - NLT).

To these [men] He also showed Himself alive after His suffering [in Gethsemane and on the cross], by [a series of] many infallible proofs and unquestionable demonstrations, appearing to them over a period of forty days and talking to them about the things concerning the kingdom of God. (Acts 1:3 - AMP).

The Christian faith hangs or falls based on the claims of the resurrection. This was undeniable proof that Jesus was who he claimed to be. The evidence of the resurrection was not the empty cross or tomb but a living, breathing Jesus who had died but was now alive. The narrative clearly records that His death was verified, and the body was properly prepared for burial and placed in a tomb.

He was clearly dead, as evidenced by the request of the religious community to post guards so there could be no alleged resurrection through the stealing of His body.

Since it was the day of Preparation [for the Sabbath], in order to prevent the bodies from hanging on the cross on the Sabbath (for that Sabbath was a high holy day) the Jews asked Pilate to have their legs broken [to hasten death] and the bodies taken away. So the soldiers came and broke the legs of the first man, and of the other who had been crucified with Him. But when they came to Jesus and saw that He was already dead, they did not break His legs. (John 19:31-33 - AMP).

The posting of soldiers at the tomb and the sealing helped to preserve the chain of evidence. He was locked in the tomb and was not allowed to leave, nor was anyone allowed to enter. The religious leaders were taking no chances with this new sect and its leadership.

The next day, on the Sabbath, the leading priests and Pharisees went to see Pilate. They told him, "Sir, we remember what that deceiver once said while he was still alive: 'After three days I will rise from the dead.' So we request that you seal the tomb until the third day. This will prevent his disciples from coming and stealing his body and then telling everyone he was raised from the dead! If that happens, we'll be worse off than we were at first." Pilate replied, "Take guards and secure it the best you can." So they sealed the tomb and posted guards to protect it. (Matthew 27:62-66 - NLT).

By their actions, the Priests and the Pharisees ensured that the body could not and would not be stolen under the guise of resurrection. It took both a phenomenal and supernatural occurrence to free Jesus from the tomb. What is in God's plan cannot be prevented by man. The evidence of the resurrection has nothing to do with a dead stolen body but rather a living body that had been previously certified dead, came alive of its own accord, and walked out, living and breathing.

The words of Jesus were not only remembered but carefully rehearsed amongst the religious leaders to the extent that they were unwilling to leave anything to chance. They were quite skeptical of His sayings regarding coming alive after three days but still secured the place of the burial to avoid any skullduggery. They were still terrified of His influence and felt that even under false pretense, the body could not be allowed to leave the tomb. They feared a greater spread of the Christian faith should this happen and continued loss of numbers from Judaism to this new sect. God is never glorified through hoaxes. False witnesses are never a part of His divine plan. God was not going to use human ingenuity to accomplish His purpose, but rather His omnipotence was going to be on display. This had to be a miracle far greater than that of Lazarus or Jairus' daughter being raised from the dead. The results of this resurrection would procure man's eternal redemption. No attempt of man could foil this spectacular display of God's power. It took Jesus to raise Lazarus from the dead, but Jesus got Himself up from the dead by the power of the Holy Spirit.

"All right," Jesus replied. "Destroy this temple, and in three days I will raise it up." "What!" they exclaimed. "It has taken forty-six years to build this Temple, and you can rebuild it in three days?" But when Jesus said "this temple," he meant his own body. (John 2:19-21 - NLT).

They failed to understand that the proof of resurrection had nothing to do with man but everything to do with God. Whereas man's condition occasioned it, God's love and power procured it. It was the sovereign power of God that was going to be responsible for orchestrating the resurrection. The stealing or hiding of the body would not be sufficient; it had to be living, breathing evidence to be classified as resurrection. God was not going to fail or come up short.

I also pray that you will understand the incredible greatness of God's power for us who believe him. This is the same mighty power that raised Christ from the dead and seated him in the place of honor at God's right hand in the heavenly realms. Now he is far above any ruler or authority or power or leader or anything else—not only in this world but also in the world to come. (Ephesians 1:19-21 - NLT).

UTTERANCE AND WITNESS

"John baptized with water, but in just a few days you will be baptized with the Holy Spirit." So when the apostles were with Jesus, they kept asking him, "Lord, has the time come for you to free Israel and restore our kingdom?" He replied, "The Father alone has the authority to set those dates and times, and they are not for you to know. But you will receive power when the Holy Spirit comes upon you. And you will be my witnesses, telling people about me everywhere—in Jerusalem, throughout Judea, in Samaria, and to the ends of the earth." (Acts 1:5-8 - NLT).

And everyone present was filled with the Holy Spirit and began speaking in other languages, as the Holy Spirit gave them this ability. At that time there were devout Jews from
...ery nation living in Jerusalem. When they heard the loud
...eryone came running, and they were bewildered to
...languages being spoken by the believers.
...amazed. "How can this be?" they
...ll from Galilee, and yet we
...languages! (Acts 2:4-

...g communities,
...d as the initial
...th the Holy Ghost.
...pirit has been tied to
...physical evidence.

There are two very compelling and provoking thoughts to consider in the Acts 2 passage. The first is indeed the phenomenon of being empowered to speak a language that was never learned to bring witness to native speakers of the language. The second is that despite the size of the crowd and the number of persons speaking, every man heard the message in his own language. The Holy Spirit gave the disciples utterance or the words to speak but also ensured that the listening audience would only hear the message in their language. It is like the Holy Spirit filtered the noise or the sounds so they only heard what they needed to, and so were not confused but enlightened. Thus, the agency of the Holy Spirit was crucial in this communication. The speakers were ignorant of the language they spoke, but those to whom the discourse was directed not only understood but were convicted by what they heard. The message heard and received spoke to the wonderful works of God. This was God revealing Himself through supernaturally gifting the Apostles to communicate to the people in their own language.

Jesus had clearly indicated that the main emphasis of bei
filled was to offer witness (prolonged public testimony).
message in tongues concerning the wonderful works
was clear evidence of that supernatural empo
Jerusalem now became the focal point whe
language-speaking Jews had gathered for Pente
Holy Spirit seized the moment to minister
them through human agents who were no
of the language that was being dispensed

And everyone present was filled with the Holy Spirit and began speaking in other languages, as the Holy Spirit gave them this ability. (Acts 2:4 - NLT).

The commission clearly states that we should go into all the world and preach the gospel. In this instance, through a unique set of circumstances, both religious and cultural, various language-speaking Jews had been brought to Jerusalem to be witnesses of this spectacular display of God's power.

The overwhelming evidence was both in the miracle of speaking and hearing. The unique empowerment of the Spirit imparted an ability to speak a known language they had never learned. But of great significance is the fact that it was not gibberish or unintelligible speech but a message that spoke about the God who had provided this witness. The Spirit's testimony concerning Jesus was clear and provided a unique platform for Christian witness, highlighting the point that the main emphasis of being filled with the Holy Spirit is to offer Christian witness. Being filled represents an empowerment that facilitates the kind of ministry that puts God on display. The Holy Spirit reserves the right to determine what manifestation will result from the infilling.

The message of the Spirit is always directed to human agents and requires a response. For a witness to be effective, the hearers must understand what is being said. An unknown tongue would not have borne fruit at Pentecost. The very structure of the message was the purview and responsibility of the Holy Spirit.

"But I will send you the Advocate—the Spirit of truth. He will come to you from the Father and will testify all about me. And you must also testify about me because you have been with me from the beginning of my ministry. (John 15: 26-27 - NLT).

RECEIVING THE HOLY SPIRIT

Even as Peter was saying these things, the Holy Spirit fell upon all who were listening to the message. The Jewish believers who came with Peter were amazed that the gift of the Holy Spirit had been poured out on the Gentiles, too. For they heard them speaking in other tongues and praising God. Then Peter asked, "Can anyone object to their being baptized, now that they have received the Holy Spirit just as we did?" (Acts 10:44-47 - NLT).

The evidence of this group of Gentiles receiving the Holy Spirit is listed as "other tongues." The disciples concurred that what they were witnessing was like that which they themselves had received and embraced. In the first instance in Acts 2, the tongues witnessed to the unbelieving community, but in this instance, it served to witness and affirm the inclusion of the Gentiles into the body of Christ. There was no doubting the genuineness of their conversion; it was evident for all to see.

Evidence of the Spirit in operation resulted in the breaking down of racial barriers and stereotypes to create an atmosphere of inclusion. It is the work of the Spirit to place believers into the body of Jesus Christ.

The human body has many parts, but the many parts make up one whole body. So it is with the body of Christ. Some of us are Jews, some are Gentiles, some are slaves, and some are free. But we have all been baptized into one body by one Spirit, and we all share the same Spirit. (1 Corinthians 12:12-13 - NLT).

CHAPTER 3

SHOW ME WHERE YOU LAID HIM

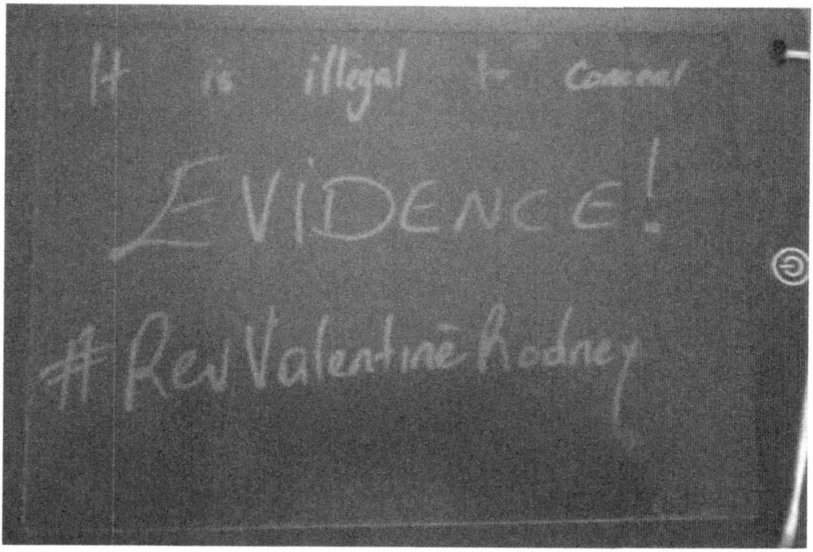

When Jesus saw her weeping and saw the other people wailing with her, a deep anger welled up within him, and he was deeply troubled. "Where have you put him?" he asked them. They told him, "Lord, come and see." Then Jesus wept. The people who were standing nearby said, "See how

much he loved him!" But some said, "This man healed a blind man. Couldn't he have kept Lazarus from dying?" (John 11:33-37 - NLT).

Jesus had already made it clear upon hearing the news of Lazarus' sickness that it was not unto death but for the glory of God that the Son of man would be glorified through it. The delay of Jesus and the subsequent death of Lazarus further complicated the matter and raised questions concerning His intervention in the matter.

Before Jesus's arrival in Bethany, Lazarus had already been certified dead, wrapped up in grave clothes, and buried in a tomb four days prior. Many persons had converged on the house. Several things needed to be present for the visible resurrection of Lazarus. The death of Lazarus had to be confirmed by the competent authority, witnesses that would testify concerning His death, an unbroken chain of custody of the body in the tomb, and the miraculous power of God to bring him back to life. This miracle put Jesus on display and brought the conversation concerning His deity to the forefront.

Jesus waited for four days; the same period Lazarus was in the tomb, because He was aware of Jewish superstition. This superstition stated that a soul stayed near the grave for three days, hoping to return to the body. It was generally accepted that after four days, there was absolutely no hope of resurrection because the soul would have departed.

Unlike Martha, Jesus was greatly moved, but His emotions were under control. There was a stark contrast in how they both wept. Whereas Martha wailed loudly, Jesus wept quietly. It is difficult to remain unaffected or detached emotional, especially when faced with a crisis being experienced by someone you love.

Jesus was troubled and angry at the scene of death and its effect on humanity. He shared in the grief of those at the tomb but was determined to do something about what had happened. In fact, this was primarily the reason why He delayed His coming. Far more was to be accomplished with Lazarus's death than would have been if he had been healed from his sickness. The pain of loss can dullen any sense of hope and expectation. Memory loss can often be associated with the grief that comes through a painful loss.

For Lazarus to be resurrected, Jesus had to be taken to where Lazarus' body was. Please note that the body came to life within the tomb unaided or assisted by any, save the command of Jesus to come forth. There was much concern about the movement of the stone, fearing that his body would have already started to decompose. Resurrection reversed any ill effects of death. The resurrected body showed no effects of having died. There was a complete and total restoration. It was as if Lazarus had never died.

The words of the detractors were silenced, and the confidence of Mary and Martha was restored. After Mary bemoaned the fact that Jesus was too late to prevent her brother from dying, He replied that he wanted access to the body. Death was not a barrier in this case but an ally. Lazarus' death was needed for Jesus to accomplish what He came to Bethany for. Sometimes, to be helped, it is needful that we face the place of our pain and discomfort. The memory of Lazarus's demise was still fresh, and to visit the place of his remains may have caused deep emotional pain, but it was necessary. Their obedience was required for the matter to be resolved. Sometimes, God does not ask us to understand His strategy but to trust His decision. They were powerless in the face of this tragedy, but Jesus was all-knowing and all-powerful.

To end the grief that they were experiencing, Jesus did not respond to her question concerning His motive in coming late but rather requested to be shown where the body was so He could extend His ministry. God does not have to remove you from the place of your pain to provide healing and support. Jesus was not going to the location to grieve but to deal with the source of their grief. Will we be honest enough to give Jesus access to the areas that have caused us the greatest level of discomfort? Even in the face of death and decay, there is still hope.

"Where have you put him?" he asked them. They told him, "Lord, come and see." Then Jesus wept. The people who were standing nearby said, "See how much he loved him!" But some said, "This man healed a blind man. Couldn't he have kept Lazarus from dying?" Jesus was still angry as he arrived at the tomb, a cave with a stone rolled

across its entrance. "Roll the stone aside," Jesus told them. But Martha, the dead man's sister, protested, "Lord, he has been dead for four days. The smell will be terrible." Jesus responded, "Didn't I tell you that you would see God's glory if you believe?" (John 11:34-40 - NLT).

Ignorance and unbelief were incapable of affecting resurrection power. Jesus did not require the crowd to believe. He was simply there to demonstrate His sovereignty over death. Lazarus was not tasked with having faith to believe, nor could he because he was dead.

The removal of the stone was natural, but the resurrection of Lazarus was supernatural. Jesus' power went beyond that of human agency. The resurrection could not be confirmed if the stone was still in place. Rolling away the stone also served to authenticate that Lazarus was right where they left him and that his original state had depreciated. This could all be confirmed once the stone was rolled away, and whatever was in the tomb would now become visible.

The rolling away of the stone was going to reveal to all the evidence of death and, subsequently, the reality of the resurrection. Jesus' plan was not about leaving things as they were but to effect a transformation that was going to be visible and undeniable. The stone represented the will of man, but Jesus represented the will of the Father. Man had given up, but God was just about to begin. Once humanity was out of the way, divinity stepped in.

Note that many believed in Jesus because of the evidence of Lazarus. It is amazing how a crisis has the potential to bring God glory. Whenever God offers a solution, it draws attention to Himself, and His character is put on display. There were some in the crowd who were extremely critical of Jesus. The question on their mind was why He had not stopped Lazarus from dying since He had a ministry of healing others, including the restoration of sight. They may have thought that Lazarus's sickness was not as serious a complaint as the restoration of sight. It is important that we see things from God's perspective. Jesus had repeatedly hinted at a greater purpose afoot. Believing to see a revelation of God's glory was His common expression. When we fail to see things from God's perspective, we are destined to arrive at premature conclusions that are not in keeping with God's will and sovereignty. God is more concerned about His will than our comfort; however, He who knows all things is committed to our welfare. Let us therefore conclude that an omniscient God knows what is best for us.

Jesus did not ask the question simply because He wanted to view the place of the last remains of Lazarus. He wanted to go there to reveal God's glory and receive glory. This was not a secretive covert operation but an overt declaration of divine power and enablement. Visiting the tomb was an open act of defiance. Death would have no power in the presence of Him, who is the resurrection and the life. He dared to believe that this was not going to be the end of Lazarus. He who had died must live again. Jesus had given His Word both to the sisters and the disciples. What appeared permanent was going to be proven temporary.

Jesus could have spoken anywhere outside of Bethany, and the job would have been done, but the credit would not have been given to Him. He was using this as an all-out effort to declare Himself to be the Messiah, the Son of the living God. There had to be witnesses to this spectacular display of God's power that would silence the critics and the cynics. The talk must now be backed up with action.

The voice of the critics was loud but not discerning. Their words paraded their ignorance concerning the work and worth of Jesus. They all concluded that it was too late and He was incompetent. Finally, a situation had arisen over which He had no authority.

The people who were standing nearby said, "See how much he loved him!" But some said, "This man healed a blind man. Couldn't he have kept Lazarus from dying?" (John 11:36-37 - NLT).

They failed to understand divine perspective. Jesus' intent and purpose was not to prevent Lazarus from dying but rather to raise him from the dead. Jesus saw hope when they were swimming in despair. He knew that His assignment was clear, and their unbelief could not prevent the miracle from occurring. It is not us who direct the situation but God. The final determiner of the outcome was not left to the bystanders with their doubts but to Christ Himself. It is not what He should have done but what is God's will. Healing a sick Lazarus would never have brought the weight of glory as did his resurrection. They were concerned with preservation whilst Jesus was concerned with transformation that would lead to resurrection.

The gathered multitude was going to lend credence to the identification of Lazarus; that he had died and his burial was clarified and verified. He was wrapped in grave clothes prepared for burial and then laid in the tomb. Many could attest to his sickness and subsequent death. Resurrection would require the same body to return from the dead with full faculties and not showing any signs of decay. What was deemed an irreversible process was now being confronted by the omnipotent one.

So they rolled the stone aside. Then Jesus looked up to heaven and said, "Father, thank you for hearing me. You always hear me, but I said it out loud for the sake of all these people standing here, so that they will believe you sent me." Then Jesus shouted, "Lazarus, come out!" And the dead man came out, his hands and feet bound in graveclothes, his face wrapped in a headcloth. Jesus told them, "Unwrap him and let him go!" (John 11:41-44 - NLT).

The only thing that human competence could address at the tomb was the barrier they had been placed there, not so much to keep Lazarus in but to keep the stench from getting out. Man's extremity requires God's divinity to deal with the limitation. They could roll away the stone, but only Jesus could give life, reversing the effects of death. The rolling away of the stone signified the birthing of hope. Jesus had no fear or trepidation that He was doing the right thing. The sting of death was going to be removed, and the fear replaced with confidence in the Resurrector. The stone was rolled away so the resurrection would be visible to all those who had a view of the tomb. They would see Lazarus being raised by the words of the Lord Jesus Christ.

Jesus was about to transform the place of grief and disappointment into a place of power and joy. The great enemy called death was about to be conquered. He wanted to correct the injustice that death had done to the relationships that people shared. Jesus was going to reconnect what death had severed. It is evident from the text that Jesus can always do something no matter how dire the circumstances are.

DON'T TAMPER WITH THE EVIDENCE

When all the people heard of Jesus' arrival, they flocked to see him and also to see Lazarus, the man Jesus had raised from the dead. Then the leading priests decided to kill Lazarus, too, for it was because of him that many of the people had deserted them and believed in Jesus. (John 12:9-11 – NLT).

God has a way of delivering us from evil expectations. Not everyone who has witnessed your elevation is supportive.

There are those with the sentiment that you are either undeserving or it's an affront to their desires.
You can make many plans, but the LORD's purpose will prevail. (Proverbs 19:21 - NLT).

There were many witnesses to the resurrection of Lazarus from the dead. Countless others had heard the report and were desirous of seeing the evidence of this phenomenal miracle that was witnessed. The proof of the resurrection still abounded in the living breathing person of Lazarus. This singular act redounded to the fame of Jesus, and many were moved to reconsider their view of Him. The entire community and adjacent environs were abuzz with this spectacular display of God's power. Many, no doubt, would have been reciting stories concerning the claims of Jesus, which were even now being fully substantiated before their eyes. This miracle was not done in secret before a private believing or cultic audience, but it was open and visible to the entire mourning community that had gathered in Bethany at that time because of Lazarus' death.

There were far too many witnesses for the religious leaders to discount what had happened. In fact, the proof of the resurrection was still evident, and it disrupted their plans to minimise the importance of Jesus and His ministry.

This was disconcerting to the religious community that began to experience attrition. They now decided to plot to kill Lazarus to get rid of the evidence. What they failed to recognise was that the miracle could not be withdrawn. It had already occurred and was witnessed by many. The evidence of your testimony is unstoppable. The killing of Lazarus would not prevent Jesus from receiving glory. The work had been done, and the mission accomplished. Jesus was not just talk; He was about performance and irrefutable evidence.

We must never fail to show people the evidence or tangible proof of God's intervention in our lives. The evidence will point more to God at work than how deserving we are. Lazarus had nothing to do with the miracle he received; it was all about God's sovereignty and a phenomenal display of His power.

Notice that they believed in Jesus because of the miracle and did not try to deify the recipient of the miracle. The evidence pointed to Jesus, the Messiah and Miracle Worker. It was irrefutable and above and beyond any contradictions.

Destroying the evidence cannot undo what has already happened or erase it from the minds of those who saw. Once you have witnessed a miracle, you cannot unsee it. Killing Lazarus would only serve to further expose their insecurities and unwillingness to affirm the irrefutable evidence of Jesus being Messiah.

Despite the hostility expressed towards Lazarus, he was not fearfully hiding. The miracle he had experienced gave him boldness and reaffirmed his faith in Jesus. It became not just a talking point but a rallying point for witness. His experience was a clear demonstration relating to the deity of Christ. It is amazing that this notable miracle attracted both positive and negative feedback.

May our lives produce the evidence that will facilitate the coming to faith of many. God can produce supernatural manifestations without anyone trying to falsify the evidence to help Him. Being dishonest and disingenuous is never consistent with integrity in witness. Supernatural manifestations are consistent with God's will; we don't need to plant evidence or recruit actors to present false claims. Evidence always has a magnetic quality or ability to draw persons to a specified location based on curiosity and a need to verify or confirm the claims. It is evident that people not only wanted to hear, they wanted to see and experience. Being in the presence of Lazarus was undeniable confirmation as he represented the evidence that a resurrection had taken place. So, the excitement was intensified because both the resurrected and the Resurrector were at the same location.

The resurrection of Lazarus caused a mass exodus from Judaism to this new burgeoning faith. It provided to many the undeniable evidence they needed to substantiate the deity of Christ. Change, even in the face of overwhelming evidence, can still be daunting. Sometimes, there is a preference with sticking to the known rather than venturing out into the unknown.

Sometimes, the big question is not one of believing but being so dogmatic in your current beliefs that you are unwilling to entertain any other belief, even with the evidence staring you in the face. Supporting the familiar and rejecting without any objective consideration the new and different seemed to be a favourite pastime of the Scribes and Pharisees. But the religious community went a step further. Not only was there a blunt refusal to consider any other option, but plans were also implemented to prevent others from embracing the new way.

"What sorrow awaits you teachers of religious law and you Pharisees. Hypocrites! For you shut the door of the Kingdom of Heaven in people's faces. You won't go in yourselves, and you don't let others enter either. (Matthew 23:23 - NLT).

It is illegal to withhold evidence even from those not supporting you or your claims. Lazarus was the living embodiment of something supernatural that had occurred. He was the evidence that resurrection was possible, and Jesus is the Resurrector. It became clear that resurrection was not determined by place or time but by Jesus. A living Lazarus represented infallible proof of resurrection.

Their desire to kill Lazarus reflected their folly. There were just too many eyewitnesses for this evidence to be tampered with. This was not false but verifiable true. The truth simply could not be resisted or twisted.

CHAPTER 4

POWER OF CORPORATE PRAYERS

So Peter was kept in prison, but fervent and persistent prayer for him was being made to God by the church. The very night before Herod was to bring him forward, Peter was sleeping between two soldiers, bound with two chains, and sentries were in front of the door guarding the prison. Suddenly, an angel of the Lord appeared [beside him] and a light shone in the cell. The angel struck Peter's side and awakened him, saying, "Get up quickly!" And the chains fell off his hands. The angel said to him, "Prepare yourself and strap on your sandals [to get ready for whatever may happen]." And he did so. Then the angel told him, "Put on your robe and follow me." And Peter went out following the angel. He did not realize that what was being done by the angel was real, but thought he was seeing a vision. When they had passed the first guard and the second, they came to the iron gate that leads into the city. Of its own accord it swung open for them; and they went out and went along one street, and at once the angel left him. When Peter came to his senses, he said, "Now I know for certain that the

Lord has sent His angel and has rescued me from the hand of Herod and from all that the Jewish people were expecting [to do to me]." When he realized what had happened, he went to the house of Mary the mother of John, who was also called Mark, where many [believers] were gathered together and were praying continually [and had been praying all night]. (Acts 12:5-12 – AMP).

As news of my hospitalization spread, and even in the face of limited available information, centers of prayer worldwide were lit. Local churches abandoned their regular programming, and some went on a 24-hour prayer watch, the main thrust being to pray for my recovery and return to good health.

It was as if a match had been lit, becoming a raging inferno of passionate and sustained prayer engagement with the Almighty. The phrase on most lips was "No, this will not end in death, but we will have the evidence of answered prayer." In several online programs, the same fervour was demonstrated to the point where fasts were called, and the Christian community was summoned to intercede.

God was using this situation as a summons to gather His people into the secret place. The Christian community once again demonstrated that we are more united than we are divided. Denominational differences were certainly not a barrier or deterrent. Clearly, we all believed in the same God and were wholly reliant upon Him. Even in some office spaces, time was allowed for gatherings just to offer prayers.

What occasioned this prayer saturation paled compared to the God now receiving due attention and notice. It appeared as if a universal summons had been issued, and volunteers had unanimously appeared to answer the call.

Both individual and corporate prayers were being offered in response to the SOS. Based on the nature of my illness, I was in and out of consciousness and could not pray as I wanted, but God raised up an army of intercessors to bear the burden. Their prayers, like incense, ascended to the heavens and caught the attention of the Almighty. They prayed in droves and in hope, expectation, and anticipation that the evidence of answered prayer would present as infallible proof that the real power in prayer is the God who answers.

It must never be misconstrued that during the incarceration of James, the church was not in prayer mode. Prayer and the study of the Word were always major ingredients of the apostolic way and had become the lifestyle of the believing community. The suggestion here is that the prayer levels escalated with the rise in threat level. It would be true to say that intercession was intensified. They prayed without ceasing. Let us also be aware that prayer may not avert adversity but still accomplish God's will. Whereas certain administrative responsibilities were delegated to others by the apostles, they saw prayer as one of their core functions that could be encouraged but not delegated. To the infant, church prayer was a matter of priority.

Their continuance in prayer is a clear indication that their reverence for God was greater than their fear of men. With intense prayer, there is always the belief that God will provide opportunities during times of adversity. Adversity will never cause God's mission for His people to be aborted.

The reports of focused prayer came from so many countries, too numerous to mention. Even after my discharge from the hospital, many groups and individuals continued in prayer because they did not just want me to be healed but rather to be made whole.

DAILY ROUTINE

The daily routine at the Trillium Health Partners Hospital in Mississauga consisted of bloodwork every morning. I would be awakened by a nurse's voice informing me that it was time for my bloodwork. This consisted of either utilizing the existing IVs or establishing a new one. The blood was subsequently drawn into tubes and sent to the lab for analysis to determine the next treatment phase. My blood pressure was taken at regular intervals automatically and electronically recorded.

Then would come the dreaded breakfast mealtime with choices on the tray, but there was nothing particularly interesting as far as my dietary preferences were concerned. Alongside the meal were three types of medication for blood pressure and pain. It would also be time for my routine stomach injection of blood thinners. "It will only be a small sting" was the often repeated statement, which certainly did not make it any easier.

I was also subjected to routine CT scans to determine the level of progress being made in the brain. This required my bed to be wheeled to the ground floor where this was done.

My daily analysis was not just medical but included questioning at odd hours to determine my focus and cognition level. These questions included but were not limited to "What is your name?", "Where are you?", "Why are you here?" and "What is today's date?" The only question that would pose a challenge every now and again was the date. I simply lost track of time, whether date or time of day. Not to mention the routine exercises that were done: the movement of the feet and each hand was used to squeeze the nurse's hand to test its strength. I was also asked to use my finger to touch my nose and then subsequently the finger of the nurse and back.

They brought a speech therapist once, but was considered not needed as I was always very coherent. I was under 24-hour-a-day monitoring in the ICU and had a signal button close at hand should I require the services of a nurse or critical care worker.

THE SUPERNATURAL VISITATION

This almost did not get written, as I had totally forgotten about it. During a discussion with my publisher, Cleveland

McLeish, he asked if, during the hospitalization, based on the nature of the illness, I had an out-of-body experience. This became the cue for me to remember an incident that occurred whilst I was in the ICU at THP Mississauga.

My long-time friend and ministry colleague indicated that my godson and another young person wanted to pay me a visit, to which I consented. After a few attempts, we settled on Saturday, the 20th of April 2024. We had a very solid discussion, and if I would say so, time of ministry.

Towards the end of the visit, I saw a lady walking into the room in scrubs with nothing in her hands, and she began setting up a dome in a section of the room. She was very businesslike, and this never felt at all like an intrusion but rather someone with expertise fulfilling an assignment. My godson and the other guest were completely oblivious to what was transpiring. The dome emitted various coloured lights, and I somehow understood that this was supposed to be therapeutic, which caused me to relax. Could it be that I was transported into another supernatural dimension with the intent of making me whole? The room, by then, appeared to be more spacious, and it was almost like you could see everything at once.

And God never said to any of the angels, "Sit in the place of honor at my right hand until I humble your enemies, making them a footstool under your feet." Therefore, angels are only servants—spirits sent to care for people who will inherit salvation. (Hebrews 1:13-14 - NLT).

Angels are ministering spirits that are released on assignment by the Lord to do His bidding. Believers are not the ones to release angels on assignment or to command them to obey their commands. We have a responsibility to call upon God, as were the multitudes across the globe who had lifted their voices in intercession on my behalf. We must, however, understand that a sovereign God will decide how He chooses to intervene or respond to the cries of His children.

Like Peter in Acts 12, I can testify that God sent His holy angel to deliver me. The doctors are due commendation for doing their best, but there is an aspect of my becoming whole that was entrusted only to the hands of the Almighty. This visitation allowed me to access the supernatural help required to effect the needed transformation.

If you make the LORD your refuge, if you make the Most High your shelter, no evil will conquer you; no plague will come near your home. For he will order his angels to protect you wherever you go. They will hold you up with their hands so you won't even hurt your foot on a stone. (Psalm 91:9-12 - NLT).

There is much debate concerning whether it was an actual angel or a legend regarding the healings by the Pool of Bethesda. However, what can be said to be true is that the events were not natural but supernatural.

Now there is at Jerusalem by the sheep market a pool, which is called in the Hebrew tongue Bethesda, having five porches. In these lay a great multitude of impotent folk, of blind, halt, withered, waiting for the moving of the water. For an angel went down at a certain season into the pool, and troubled the water: whosoever then first after the troubling of the water stepped in was made whole of whatsoever disease he had. (John 5:2-4 - KJV).

The interaction of angels with man is well documented and cannot be rationally disputed. Consideration must be given to the view that it is God who determines their job description, and He can assign them at any time to carry out His will without seeking our approval. Doing the Father's bidding and fulfilling His will is the direct responsibility of angels as they are released to minister to humanity. God can, whenever He choses, invade our reality or bring us into dimensions that we have no knowledge of its existence to give us an existential experience. It is God who choses the time and place of these supernatural encounters and the purposes of them.

A sudden calm invaded the room, and I felt an overwhelming peace, and all the discomforts became a distant memory. She left as quietly as she came, not interacting with any of us but just seemed bent on fulfilling her assignment. I felt at that time that she knew perfectly what she was there to do and performed it with great skill and ease.

She did not look like any of the staff members I had previously seen and interacted with. Once they came on shift, staff members would normally introduce themselves to me by name and indicate what shift they were there to work on. Coupled with that, the names of the workers on the various shifts would also be written on the patient board.

I was aware that my comfort level had risen to an all-time high, and snuggling up under the blanket, I drifted off to sleep. My godson stated that only a doctor came into the room to check on my vitals and then left. He was not aware of or had seen anyone else. Spiritual awareness is often specific and received by the intended audience, irrespective of who is present.

It is possible to share a physical location but not have the same supernatural experience. Whoever God wants to be affected will have the experience. We see something quite vivid in Paul's supernatural conversion on the road to Damascus.

"As I was on the road, approaching Damascus about noon, a very bright light from heaven suddenly shone down around me. I fell to the ground and heard a voice saying to me, 'Saul, Saul, why are you persecuting me?' "'Who are you, lord?' I asked. "And the voice replied, 'I am Jesus the Nazarene, the one you are persecuting.' The people with me saw the light but didn't understand the voice speaking to me. (Acts 22:6-9 - NLT).

To my surprise, on Sunday morning, when I awoke, there was no sign of the globe. It had vanished without a trace. Only the memory of what I had seen the previous night lingered. I also never saw that nurse again, which was quite a mystery. This was also the day scheduled for a CT scan to determine whether the drain could be taken out and the staples removed from my head, along with determining a date for my discharge.

There was talk from the medical personnel that they wanted me to be discharged but were awaiting this scan to arrive at a conclusion. The scan consequently indicated that it was now safe for these procedures to be done. They had initially indicated that I would leave that hospital to return to Brampton Hospital from which I had come. There was also talk about whether I would need rehab and physiotherapy.

When they inquired of Brampton Hospital, no bed could be located for me at that time. To me, it seemed that what had happened the previous night could well have been an angelic visitation. It was almost as if an angel was dispatched to my room to facilitate the Father's will.

It is amazing how my rate of recovery improved significantly after that encounter. I now understand that much experimentation has been taking place regarding the use of lights to enhance therapy, especially in critical care situations. After the visitation, things began to move rapidly, resulting in my being told that upon discharge, I would not be going to Brampton Hospital or be recommended for either rehabilitation or physiotherapy. It would also be true to state that all the signs the doctors were looking for to arrange for my discharge happened within the week after the visitation. I was subsequently moved from the ICU to a regular ward one floor up because of the rapid rate of recovery.

I simply stand in awe of both the wisdom and power of God and His ability to do exceedingly abundantly and above all that we can ask or think. This was reminiscent of how the apostles in the book of Acts would have angelic visitations under dire circumstances. It is apparent that there was an invasion of the supernatural that ultimately served the purposes of God with respect to His servant.

The fight is far from over, and the assignment is far from finished. Only eternity will unfold the full extent of the angelic assignment. God has a way of saving His anointed from the destructive devices of the enemy. The prayer covering does not end with recovering from the trauma of the sickness but must also relate to the future assignments that God has in store for His servant.

My prayer is like that of the Apostle Paul. We must attach the same level of urgency and importance to prayers whether in or outside the hospital.

Devote yourselves to prayer with an alert mind and a thankful heart. Pray for us, too, that God will give us many opportunities to speak about his mysterious plan concerning

Christ. That is why I am here in chains. Pray that I will proclaim this message as clearly as I should. (Colossians 4:2-4 - NLT).

There is a wide-open door for a great work here, although many oppose me. (1 Corinthians 16:9 - NLT).

God will take you through the trauma of an experience to prepare and equip you for future assignments that will require tenacity, strength, and discernment. The experience contains a message to all that nothing shall be impossible with God and, to me, that the divine intervention was to give me more time to complete my assignment here on earth. Both my voice and presence are required in places at a specific time according to God's divine time schedule.

CHAPTER 5

D-DAY (DISCHARGE)

The final set of CT scans had been done. The drain and staples were removed and it was the final day of my admittance. The routine checks had been done, and the discharge procedure was now on in earnest. The greatest relief was to see the remnants of the ECG patches and the IV being removed. It was truly liberating, and I felt like one phase of the journey was over, and a new one began. There was still the white sticky substance from where the bandages were on my forehead, arms, and hands to be dealt with.

There were also numerous dead cells that seemed to cover me like a cloud of dust on my head and body. My wife tried her best to remove the dead cells, but they just seemed to increase in quantity.

I was ecstatic when the wheelchair was brought into the room, and my wife, with documentation in hand, walked with me to the entrance. We were singing the song "I have a very good God ooo." There was a welcomed shift in the atmosphere on coming out of the hospital that had housed me for almost three weeks.

Pastor Sophia Martin was on the scene, and we bundled up in the vehicle with smiles of jubilation. As she drove away amidst the excitement, we raised the anthem to God again:

I have A very Big God
A Very Big God Oh
E no dae Fall my Hand O
He's always on my Side O
A very Big God.

See my Life
Nar so, so Wonder
If you know my God
He's a Miracle Worker
E Dae come through on a Regular
Everything na Jabarata
Him Blessings no need Formula
This my God
He's A very Big God.[1]

The song resonated and bore testimony to how we felt about His operations and involvement in our lives. The air felt crisp, and I drank deeply from all the exciting sounds and sights outside. It all seemed so new and stood in contrast to

---

[1] https://www.wmlyrics.com/tim-godfrey-big-god-lyrics-ft-anderson/

the hospital room I had just been released from. It took some time for my eyes to adjust to the sunlight outside. I had to blink several times because of the brightness. It all felt strange, but a welcomed change it was.

When God is doing a work, it can often fall well outside the realms of human comprehension.

"My thoughts are nothing like your thoughts," says the LORD. "And my ways are far beyond anything you could imagine. For just as the heavens are higher than the earth, so my ways are higher than your ways and my thoughts higher than your thoughts." (Isaiah 55:8-9 - NLT).

WALKING IN HIS PRESENCE

Shortly after being discharged from the hospital, Elder Stanberry indicated that my hair needed to be shaved down to one level. The hospital had shaved off half of the hair on my head in preparation for the surgery. On a day agreed upon, all the hair was shaved off, presenting me with a whole new look.

With the regrowth of the hair, a decision was made to attend a barber salon to trim and shave. Walking from the vehicle to the barber shop and vice versa was a task. Even though I had gained some measure of mobility, it was still challenging.

I was in need of some supplies, so Elder Stanberry took me to an African product store. On entering the store, the owner, an African, kept acknowledging and bowing before me. We struck up a discussion with him indicating that I looked African, to which I remarked that I had been referred to as Ghanian.

To this, he retorted, "You are Igbo." He kept saying that I brought a presence into the store and there was something about me. He then said he would offer me a gift. He indicated that it was the first time someone had stepped into the store, and he felt like that. He was clearly implying some supernatural connection.

He helped us select the products I needed, showing me which he considered the best in the range. I was given a brief lecture concerning the tribe (Igbo), which he figured I came from in Nigeria. He mentioned that they were into economics, businesspeople, and were particularly wealthy. I just stood there listening keenly to all he said and somehow wondering why all of this now.

The conversation culminated with him deciding to honour me with a gift from the range of products he carried, all while indicating something special about me. Listening to him, I got the impression that the entire spiritual atmosphere in the shop had shifted positively, and he felt that my presence there had something to do with it.

I never bothered to ask whether we were from the same faith or not. What struck me was how attuned he was to the spiritual realm. He thanked me profusely for coming into the store as he figured something supernatural had transpired. The level of reverence—almost awe—that he treated me with was reminiscent of when I was in Uganda doing ministry and was being greeted by Christian leaders and laity alike.

It was amazing that during that time, he never really engaged with Elder; the focus was entirely on me. The whole encounter was surreal, and it almost felt like God had dispatched angels to me that kept accompanying me wherever I went.

I vividly recall that, over two decades previously, I had a meeting at the West End Church of God of Prophecy, where we witnessed a very special visitation on Sunday morning. Many were brought to their knees, having encountered the awesome presence of God. Immediately after the service, a teenager told me that during my time of ministry, she saw two angels, one on either side of me, and the Lord told her that no evil would be able to harm me. That day, we all knew we had received a supernatural encounter. It had nothing to do with my preaching but everything to do with God who had timed that visitation.

I left the church with a renewed boldness that God was with me and that He would cause me to triumph in any power encounter situation. I was unafraid as I ventured into ministry to engage the supernatural. This was not just surreal; it felt like an epiphany. One phase of ministry was now closed, and a whole new phase had begun.

If others could see the operations of God on me, then I would be left with no other option but to believe that this was indeed the dawning of a new day.

CHAPTER 6

SHOW ME THE EVIDENCE

Doubt can still exist, even when presented with irrefutable evidence. Willful ignorance does not minimize the significance of the weight of evidence presented. A crisis can undermine our faith and confidence, causing us to lose both heart and hope. However, a crisis can cause us to repose greater trust and confidence in God in light of an understanding of our frailty and finiteness and, indeed, God's sovereignty coupled with His omniscience, omnipresence, and omnipotence.

But very early on Sunday morning the women went to the tomb, taking the spices they had prepared. They found that the stone had been rolled away from the entrance. So they went in, but they didn't find the body of the Lord Jesus. As they stood there puzzled, two men suddenly appeared to them, clothed in dazzling robes. The women were terrified and bowed with their faces to the ground. Then the men asked, "Why are you looking among the dead for someone who is alive? He isn't here! He is risen from the dead!

Remember what he told you back in Galilee, that the Son of Man must be betrayed into the hands of sinful men and be crucified, and that he would rise again on the third day." (Luke 24:1-7 - NLT).

The tragedy of the crucifixion tended to overshadow thoughts of resurrection. The women going to the tomb to anoint Jesus' body with spices was a clear indication that they expected a body to be there. The women were simply carrying out the Jewish tradition of anointing with spices that accompanied burial. The intention showed love and devotion but was fraught with spiritual blindness and ignorance concerning Christ fulfilling His purpose. The revelation behind His teachings had become obscure, totally eluding them. A heightened state of emotion can sometimes numb our spiritual senses and cause a tailspin of ignorance.

On arrival at the tomb, the women discovered that it was empty, and they received a message from two angels there. The message spoke volumes to what had preceded their arrival. Resurrection had taken place, and the body of evidence was at large. Jesus was on the move and had gone into a place where they were to meet up with Him afterward.

Resurrection was based on a physical and not a spiritual re-appearance. The body that died must be the one that is raised. There could be no doubt whatsoever that they were one and the same. It is amazing that the resurrected body was going to bear the physical marks imposed upon it prior to death, namely that of the piercing with the nails and the sword wounds in the sides.

The women came to complete a task that had been done hastily with regard to preparing the body of Jesus for burial. Their coming would also have refuted the claims that the body had been stolen. However, they were wondering how to solve the problem of the stone blocking the tomb's entrance.

To their astonishment, the stone in question had been rolled away, granting access to the tomb. The women would not have been strong enough to overcome the guards or remove the stone, hence the nature of their discussions. Considering the circumstances, I am unsure if there would have been individuals willing to volunteer. However, the scriptures are explicit that an angel of the Lord had rolled the stone away subsequent to a great earthquake.

Suddenly there was a great earthquake! For an angel of the Lord came down from heaven, rolled aside the stone, and sat on it. His face shone like lightning, and his clothing was as white as snow. The guards shook with fear when they saw him, and they fell into a dead faint. (Matthew 28:2-4 - NLT).

The rolling away of the stone was not to let Jesus out but so that others could see and bear witness to the fact that He was no longer in the tomb. The resurrected body of Jesus could pass through material barriers.

That Sunday evening the disciples were meeting behind locked doors because they were afraid of the Jewish leaders. Suddenly, Jesus was standing there among them! "Peace be with you," he said. (John 20:19 - NLT).

The women were not expecting to find an empty tomb or the stone rolled away. The angels announced to the women, "Why do you seek the living among the dead?" The angels appeared to be surprised that the women were surprised at the unfolding sequence of events. They reminded the women of what Jesus had said concerning His resurrection on the third day, and then they remembered. They, therefore, went to the eleven to proclaim the resurrection of the Lord Jesus Christ.

They did not immediately believe, considering the statement to be a tale. At that time, the testimony of women was not deemed credible or authoritative. The position of despair of the disciple's post-crucifixion made it even harder to believe. They were utterly skeptical. The road to transformation and acceptance required evidence. Peter ran to confirm and saw perfectly folded grave clothes and an empty tomb. It appeared like a scene where the body had disappeared, leaving the clothing behind as evidence of what once was.

As they sat down to eat, he took the bread and blessed it. Then he broke it and gave it to them. Suddenly, their eyes were opened, and they recognized him. And at that moment he disappeared! (Luke 24:30-31 - NLT).

The revelation of the resurrected Lord was made even more apparent as He dialogued with two disciples on the road to Emmaus. This was further confirmed by His appearance to the women and the disciples behind closed doors. This evidence required a verdict.

Withholding evidence can hinder transformation and is illegal for believers who are witnesses to the truth of the gospel message and have testimonies. All those who experienced the resurrected Lord were quick to testify, and so may we be.

SHOW YOURSELF TO THE PRIEST

As Jesus continued on toward Jerusalem, he reached the border between Galilee and Samaria. As he entered a village there, ten men with leprosy stood at a distance, crying out, "Jesus, Master, have mercy on us!" He looked at them and said, "Go show yourselves to the priests." And as they went, they were cleansed of their leprosy. One of them, when he saw that he was healed, came back to Jesus, shouting, "Praise God!" He fell to the ground at Jesus' feet, thanking him for what he had done. This man was a Samaritan. Jesus asked, "Didn't I heal ten men? Where are the other nine? Has no one returned to give glory to God except this foreigner?" And Jesus said to the man, "Stand up and go. Your faith has healed you." (Luke 17:11-19 - NLT).

Within these passages lies a narrative that speaks to faith, forgiveness, and the power of God's grace. God will selectively decide the place for a divine encounter that will radically transform your lives forever. The scope and reach of God's sovereignty and power knows no boundary and cannot be restricted. There is no challenge that is too difficult for Him.

It was in the mixed zone or border between Galilee and Samaria that this demonstration of divine power was to take place. It was a kind of no-man's territory and a wellspring of division seemingly devoid of compassion and empathy. Jesus' intentionality was exhibited here, for He was on His way to Jerusalem but arrived at the border.

God will often not wait for us to find Him but show up exactly where we are to provide for us what is most needed. He was clearly not sent for like Jairus did, but arrived to make Himself available. It is amazing that the beneficiaries of this miracle clearly reflected what constituted the population at the border. People were there vulnerable and hurting, but they were considered to be the offscouring of society and beyond the scope of medical science with respect to cures. Sometimes, your pain and discomfort can become the very means by which you are ostracised. The infectious nature of the disease caused social and religious alienation. Unlike Naaman, a cosmetic cover-up would not do because they were not considered valuable or important to society, but rather, a degrading of their humanity meant they were seen as a thing to be avoided at all costs. God's power to save and heal is not limited to any ethnic, cultural, or geographic grouping.

Within this mixed zone was a group considered to be the disenfranchised offscouring of society based on the incurable but contagious disease of leprosy that they had. They were to be avoided at all costs, and would often voice the declaration "Unclean" to warn people they encountered to stay clear due to the contagious nature of the disease.

The method of healing stands in stark contrast to that of a certain leper in Matthew 8:2-3 who was simply given an instruction to follow (wash in the pool of Siloam) to procure his healing. Upon request for healing, in this case, Jesus did the unthinkable of touching and declaring him clean. Jesus cleanses and cannot be contaminated by what affects us. This one was going to be dependent on a walk of faith and not a walk of shame.

Their cry was from a distance. They observed the relevant protocol, not using the word "unclean" to draw attention to their condition but rather a plea for help wrapped up in the word "Mercy." They saw Him as having authority over what plagued and caused them to be ostracized. Their cry was not intended for Jesus to ignore and avoid but rather for Him to come and help. They were confident that He had the ability to help by healing them. They longed to be integrated back into society as normal, functioning individuals.

Often, when we call on Jesus, His response may be to give us instructions that may appear to be illogical. Once we call, we must position ourselves to both obey and submit to His authority and instructions. He never rebuked the sicknesses or declared them well. The priest, under the Levitical law, played a vital role in diagnosing leprosy and declaring that someone was cured or healed. This was crucial if one was to be integrated back into society. The very system that rejected and labeled must now confirm their status before acceptance.

Whereas the priest could not cleanse the leper but would unwittingly confirm that the power of Christ had healed them. The priest was a professional diagnostician of leprosy, so his words would stand as it related to them being disease-free. The evidence of the cleansed lepers represented a testimony to the priests concerning the awesome power of God.

The text aptly demonstrates the relationship between faith and action. As they went, they were cleansed. But the priest's verification would allow for full integration into society. Jesus' compassion extended to them being healed and reconnecting with their loved ones. May the evidence of healing and wholeness be evident in the lives of the readers. May you see and experience the goodness of our great God in your lives.

SEEING TO BELIEVE

One of the twelve disciples, Thomas (nicknamed the Twin), was not with the others when Jesus came. They told him, "We have seen the Lord!" But he replied, "I won't believe it unless I see the nail wounds in his hands, put my fingers into them, and place my hand into the wound in his side." Eight days later the disciples were together again, and this time Thomas was with them. The doors were locked; but suddenly, as before, Jesus was standing among them. "Peace be with you," he said. Then he said to Thomas, "Put your finger here, and look at my hands. Put your hand into the wound in my side. Don't be faithless any longer. Believe!" "My Lord and my God!" Thomas exclaimed. Then Jesus told him, "You believe because you have seen me. Blessed are those who believe without seeing me." (John 20:24-29 - NLT).

Let us not be offended if, at times, others require more than just our words to corroborate a story. Rest assured that what has taken place must be verifiable. It is not the question of belief that is at risk, but we need the evidence to support and justify the claims that have been made. The disciples did not initially believe the women when they stated their belief that Jesus had been resurrected. It was only after concrete evidence that they too believed having seen and spoken to Jesus.

The Samaritan woman was told by the multitude that they came to Jesus because of her but believed in Him when He spoke to them. Each person must weigh the evidence and make an informed decision to arrive at a conclusion. Whereas it takes faith to believe and not see, it is not sinful to require evidence to believe. Requiring evidence must not be attributed to doubt but simply a means of verification. What was being reported was of such an order of magnitude that nothing could be left to chance. Thomas wanted to do his due diligence so he could speak from the position of being an eyewitness and not reporting from a third-party position.

The integrity of those who reported that Jesus had been resurrected was not questioned; rather, Thomas wanted his own experience. If all that has been reported is true, I still want to be shown and experience the evidence. He wanted to approach things from the perspective of due diligence as an act of confirmation.

Many Samaritans from the village believed in Jesus because the woman had said, "He told me everything I ever did!" When they came out to see him, they begged him to stay in their village. So he stayed for two days, long enough for many more to hear his message and believe. Then they said to the woman, "Now we believe, not just because of what you told us, but because we have heard him ourselves. Now we know that he is indeed the Savior of the world." (John 4:39-42 - NLT).

The disciples were huddled together with the doors locked. Seeing the fears represented, Thomas just needed physical evidence that the resurrection of Christ was as they had reported. He could not see with their eyes or believe with their heart. Before you chastise Thomas, just remember that this added to the chain of evidence that solidified the resurrection of Jesus. They had been eyewitnesses of what Thomas also needed to be a witness of.

Jesus did not rebuke Thomas eight days later but rather granted him his request. All aspects of doubt and unbelief were settled as Thomas received a personal encounter with the resurrected Jesus.

WORKING THE WORKS OF GOD

As Jesus was walking along, he saw a man who had been blind from birth. "Rabbi," his disciples asked him, "why was this man born blind? Was it because of his own sins or his parents' sins?" "It was not because of his sins or his parents' sins," Jesus answered. "This happened so the power of God could be seen in him. We must quickly carry out the tasks assigned us by the one who sent us. The night is coming, and then no one can work." (John 9:1-4 - NLT).

This amazing narrative is both instructional and informative. It highlights how God's power will always trump or supersede cultural norms and expectations. It is amazing that in the previous chapter, they wanted to stone Jesus, asserting that He was guilty of blasphemy. Jesus was not perturbed or disturbed by His confrontation with the religious leaders but disregarded them and their hatred. He was not in any way ruffled by their treatment.

He seemed unusually calm and confident in the presence of those who misjudged, insulted, and slandered Him. This is a quality of grace that we need to possess as evidence of a strong, committed relationship with God.

The encounter with the blind beggar would demonstrate the ongoing victory of light over darkness and God over the hapless conditions of humanity. This man was representative of all humanity that is visionless from birth. All mankind is spiritually blind and needs to be enlightened by Jesus, the Messiah, even though, in many instances, they are not very receptive. It is impossible to see without light.

The disciples' questions showed the prevailing cultural and religious beliefs of the day. Birth defects, such as blindness, were normally attributed to having their roots in the committal of sins, whether by the parents or the individual while he was in the womb. This basic assumption formed their worldview, and they were more concerned about discussing the cause of the condition rather than extending compassion. This, too, was a common established view in Judaism. Ezekiel 18:20 was used to partially substantiate their viewpoint.

The person who sins is the one who will die. The child will not be punished for the parent's sins, and the parent will not be punished for the child's sins. Righteous people will be rewarded for their own righteous behavior, and wicked people will be punished for their own wickedness. (Ezekiel 18:20 - NLT).

"Why do you quote this proverb concerning the land of Israel: 'The parents have eaten sour grapes, but their children's mouths pucker at the taste'? (Ezekiel 18:2 - NLT).

Physical infirmity was seen as a punishment for sin. Cause of death was attributed to sin. It was stated that if a pregnant woman engaged in idolatry, the foetus also commits the sin.

You must not bow down to them or worship them, for I, the LORD your God, am a jealous God who will not tolerate your affection for any other gods. I lay the sins of the parents upon their children; the entire family is affected—even children in the third and fourth generations of those who reject me. (Exodus 20:5 - NLT).

Some have attributed the jostling of the children, Esau and Jacob, in the womb as one trying to kill the other, hence prenatal sins.

But the two children struggled with each other in her womb. So she went to ask the LORD about it. "Why is this happening to me?" she asked. (Genesis 25:22 - NLT).

The disciples assumed that sin (regardless of who committed it) was the cause of the man's blindness. The disciples, like many Jews, were influenced by the interpretation of the Old

Testament called the Mishnah. Evidence of Christlikeness must be reflected not in condemning but in helping. Mercy and love must become the hallmark of our ministry. We must be less inquisitive and more practical in our approach.

The response of Jesus showed God's strategy for intervention, though not to be blamed for the cause of the affliction. The focus, therefore, shifted to what God can do rather than why. God was going to reveal Himself through the healing of this blind man. We can endure difficulties only to be supernaturally delivered by God to His credit. However, suffering had its place in revealing God's glory. What is deemed evil can further the work of God as He abolishes and conquers it. God was about to overrule in this situation by bringing an end to the man's demise through the recovery of sight.

Jesus spoke to a window of opportunity for this man and that He was going to utilise the time well as it was the time for this kind of service. Jesus was both intentional and specific in addressing the condition of this man. The use of the spittle was tied to an ancient tradition that believed the spittle of a distinguished person possessed curative powers. Jesus took the custom of the day and used it in the procurement of this miracle. The man was subsequently sent to wash in the pool of Siloam. It was not their tradition but man's obedience to the words of Jesus that brought about the miracle.

The man to be healed had to respond with faith-filled action. The miracle was only completed after full obedience. He had to find his way and trust that the God he had entrusted in would come through. This was the first instance of sight restoration in the Bible. The evidence of the work of transformation can be so significant that it becomes hard to believe that it has happened. Amazement can mean not doubting but just thinking that this is too good to be true. It is easy to be so overwhelmed by the demonstration of the power of God that it becomes impossible to explain what has been witnessed.

Those who were never witnesses of the stages of the transformation may doubt if there is a significant outcome. Regarding speculation and questioning after the miracle, the beneficiary merely stated that he was the same person who used to be the blind beggar. Whilst not fully revealing who Jesus was, he knew enough to know that He had healed him. Petty traditions and rules could not downplay the significance of what God had wrought. The man was living proof and evidence that a miracle had taken place.

It is important that we allow those who have received miracles to testify of their experiences. We can all see the same evidence but come to different conclusions. Because they perceived Jesus as a sinner, even in the face of indisputable evidence, they refused to believe. They doubted the miracle because they hated Jesus and His teachings. To them, it was easier to believe that the man was never blind than that Jesus had healed him. Sometimes it is not the works but who God uses to bring it about.

The inquiry began to verify whether it was a conspiracy involving Jesus or not. The parents, however, consented that he was born blind. The parents refused to speak further regarding how he got his sight back under the threat of excommunication. Not wanting to be trapped, they suggested that the question be posed to the recipient of the miracle.

The religious leaders wanted a truth that would not attribute anything to Jesus. They further refused to accept what should have been admissible evidence. Having refused to embrace the facts, they attempted to belittle Jesus by saying He was a sinner because He was not compliant with their man-made traditions.

The man was adamant and would not change his mind that it was Jesus' intervention that caused the restoration of his sight. Further interrogation did not cause his answer to differ, and he remained resolute even to the point of mocking their prejudice and bias.

The religious leaders despised the man and were angry because he was right and they were wrong. They did not want the truth to trump their opinions or practices. Whenever Jesus heals, it reveals. The miracles are never an end, but they are a signpost that will point others to Him.

Jesus was clearly visible but not recognisable. The contempt with which they viewed Him closed their hearts from embracing Him and His identity. The religious leaders could read the scriptures but miss the application. What you fail to admit to, you will never be released from. The problem was not the evidence; it was their mindset.

CHAPTER 7

NO GOD LIKE JEHOVAH

When I raise my powerful hand and bring out the Israelites, the Egyptians will know that I am the LORD." (Exodus 7:5 - NLT).

"Do it tomorrow," Pharaoh said. "All right," Moses replied, "it will be as you have said. Then you will know that there is no one like the LORD our God. (Exodus 8:10 - NLT).

God is about bringing order and revelation to dismantle the chaos in our lives and communities. Passive co-existence devoid of confrontation has never been God's modus operandi. Power encounters, as they are called, solidify and cement God's sovereignty overall. This will stamp the seal of His deity universally. God has no intention of becoming the best-kept or guarded secret. He desires to and has made the provisions to be known.

The heavens proclaim the glory of God. The skies display his craftsmanship. Day after day they continue to speak; night after night they make him known. (Psalm 19:1-2 - NLT).

God will disrupt and dismantle all the evil agendas of the enemy so that His people will be delivered from the evil stronghold of ignorance. God will undermine demonic strongholds and systems to bring His people into an understanding awareness of the only true God and His grace and benevolence that is extended to all of humanity.

God allowed a Hebrew child to grow up in an Egyptian household to deliver the Hebrews from Egyptian slavery and despotism. Sometimes the delay in our breakthrough is consistent with a wider agenda afoot.

When it was time for the Egyptian god's to be judged, and the demonic system of worship overthrown, God raised up Moses. God delivered him from the system to be sent back as a reformer. The Hebrews had to be delivered from a slavery mentality, and the Egyptians from their devotion to idolatry. Moses, therefore, had to fully understand the nature of his assignment and be prepared for the hostile interactions that would take place. God allowed him to be schooled in Egypt and then delivered from its system so he could deliver others from its clutches.

It is impossible to deliver anyone from the system that holds you in bondage. It is well stated that "to be free for the people, you need to be free from the people." There is a certain "coming of age" that must rationalize our decision-making. Knowing your God and knowing yourself is critically important to fulfilling your assignment.

The earth is under God's sovereignty as a unique aspect of His creation and is thus subjected to His governance and authority. He does not need or require permission to invade or settle. The evidence of God's authority on the earth is often expressed within and through His people as a witness to all.

God can and will move you from your area of study to your area of call. It is both futile and folly to resist God's will in the earth. God-backed initiatives can never fail or be ruined by societal strongholds. God desires to be known and receive worship.

God's mission in Egypt was not to annihilate the Egyptians but to reveal His presence and power. An entire community and culture were being held in bondage and needed to be delivered. The exodus was not just for the Hebrews but also for those who were seen as His nemesis. God desires to free and deliver all. Stop holding on to what God has judged and condemned. Be released to walk in the freedom that only He can provide.

Silence does not mean God is stagnant in your life. He will work subversively and then make an open declaration as His sovereign will is exposed overtly. God will conceal before He reveals. It may appear that He is static, but His intervention in your life is on schedule. He will not fail, and you will not fall. There is so much at stake that He will cause you to arise because your destiny must be fulfilled, and His glory must be put on display.

EGYPTIAN GODS AGAINST WHOM THE PLAGUES WERE POSSIBLY DIRECTED

Nile to blood	Hapi (also called Apis), the bull god, god of the Nile; Isis, goddess of the Nile; Khnum, ram god, guardian of the Nile; others.
Frogs	Heqet, goddess of birth, with a frog head.
Gnats	Set, god of the desert storms.
Flies	Re, a sun god; Uatchit, possibly represented by the fly.
Death of livestock	Hathor, goddess with a cow head; Apis, the bull god, symbol of fertility.
Boils	Sekhmet, goddess with power over disease; Sunu, the pestilence god; Isis, healing goddess.

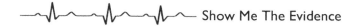

Hail	Nut, the sky goddess; Osiris, god of the crops and fertility; Set, god of the desert storms.
Locusts	Nut, the sky goddess; Osiris, god of the crops and fertility.
Darkness	Re, the sun god; Horus, a sun god; Nut, a sky goddess; Hathor, a sky goddess.
Death of firstborn	Min, god of reproduction; Heqet, goddess who attended women at childbirth; Isis, goddess who protected children; Pharaoh's firstborn son considered a god.

The plagues displayed God's judgment against the Egyptian gods and put Himself on display as the only true and living God. He was manifesting Himself to a people whose judgment was clouded by idolatry.

CHAPTER 8

BE FILLED WITH THE SPIRIT

So be careful how you live. Don't live like fools, but like those who are wise. Make the most of every opportunity in these evil days. Don't act thoughtlessly, but understand what the Lord wants you to do. Don't be drunk with wine, because that will ruin your life. Instead, be filled with the Holy Spirit, singing psalms and hymns and spiritual songs among yourselves, and making music to the Lord in your hearts. And give thanks for everything to God the Father in the name of our Lord Jesus Christ. (Ephesians 5:15-20 - NLT).

This is indeed a divine imperative and not optional. Apostle Paul was quick to point out the real evidence of a Spirit-filled life or life in the Spirit. The recognition was that both character and conduct would be affected. We are advised to be cautious and not pattern world trends and behaviour. Much wisdom must be acquired and put into effect to meet this conditionality. The believer must avail themselves of all opportunities, considering the ills and evils of society to stand out in their conduct and commitment to Christ. This commitment is wrapped up in both understanding and living according to God's will.

Living a Spirit-filled life without being empowered by the Spirit of God is virtually impossible. It is God's desire that every believer be filled with His Spirit. To make us understand that whatever fills us influences us, Paul uses drunkenness as a negative example of filling, and we are told to avoid that. Drunkenness is the negative result attributed to excessive indulgence, habitual and unrestrained indulgence of lust and sensuality. In the case of drunkenness, the person, because of the input of alcohol, loses control and becomes subject to impaired judgment and improper conduct.

However, this is in contrast to the believer being indwelt and filled with the Holy Spirit, which produces positive benefits and does not ruin your life. All believers have the Holy Spirit living within; however, the extent of His rule is determined by the Christian exercising their freedom to submit and obey to His directions for their lives. As the believer is affected, substantial changes are effected. Impaired judgment from the use of alcohol is a waste of time that leads to guilt and condemnation. When we are under the influence of the Holy Spirit, He is given access to every area of our lives so His influence can be exerted in a spiritual way. We literally become under His sovereign control and are delivered from the bondage of what would corrupt, condemn, and imprison.

Spirit-filled living is a daily choice that the believer must make to surrender themselves to the operational control of the Spirit in all aspects of their lives and activities. This will result in increased sensitivity that will prompt obedience, guidance, and submission, coupled with a dependency on the Holy Spirit's power and strength.

The main evidence of the Holy Spirit's control is revealed in the individual's character. The degree to which surrender is made is to the degree that the level of transformation is effected. Indeed, good works and faithful service are the result of being filled, yet they are not necessarily signs of being yielded to Him. Spirit-filled is primarily about character rather than action (signs and wonders). It is easier to serve the Lord in some manner than to love the unlovable or to be patient with difficult people. However, the Spirit's influence will cause Him to do through us as we cooperate what we could not do for ourselves. The believer has a choice to determine who rules over their lives by the choices they make in surrender. It is important that God be chosen over self as this will result in us experiencing the fullness of the Spirit.

Being filled with the Spirit must never be considered optional but rather intentional as we recognize it as a Biblical imperative. Serving God and coming under the influence of His Spirit must become the believer's number one priority. We must be passionate in having a strong desire for the Holy Spirit to fill us completely. This requires wholehearted trust and dependency; not resisting but becoming fully compliant and surrendered.

The focus in being filled cannot be in acquiring what you do not have but rather submitting to a unique experience with Him. The Holy Spirit testifies to us concerning our relationship with God and gives us a strong sense of identity. We belong to Christ in as much as He belongs to us.

But you are not controlled by your sinful nature. You are controlled by the Spirit if you have the Spirit of God living in you. (And remember that those who do not have the Spirit of Christ living in them do not belong to him at all.) And Christ lives within you, so even though your body will die because of sin, the Spirit gives you life because you have been made right with God. For all who are led by the Spirit of God are children of God. So you have not received a spirit that makes you fearful slaves. Instead, you received God's Spirit when he adopted you as his own children. Now we call him, "Abba, Father." For his Spirit joins with our spirit to affirm that we are God's children. (Romans 8: 9-10, 14-16 - NLT).

All believers have equal access to experience the infilling of the Holy Spirit. The imperative is quite clear: all believers should be filled with the Holy Spirit. This is not optional or just a mere suggestion. The Christo-centric life, to be successful, is dependent on this infilling. Paul indicates that what people are looking for in drinking (relaxation, escape from being unendurable, peace, and strength) can be found in life in the Spirit. For us to have a victorious walk with God, being filled is an essential part of the makeup. Being filled will allow us to stop coping and start conquering.

The Greek word for filled is the present imperative which means "be continually filled with the Spirit." This is not a one-time experience or exposure but a continuous affair. There is always the need to be continuously replenished. Filling must produce an effect. It represents empowerment for service or to produce a unique set of characteristics pre-determined by the Spirit requiring our involvement through cooperation. Education or being "spirited" is no substitute for being filled with the Spirit.

Being Spirit-filled is needed and necessary to accomplish the mission of Christ. It is possible to be literate, not liberated and consecrated but ignorant. The abiding presence of the Holy Spirit is here being referred to and not a temporary transitory experience.

"If you love me, obey my commandments. And I will ask the Father, and he will give you another Advocate, who will never leave you. He is the Holy Spirit, who leads into all truth. The world cannot receive him, because it isn't looking for him and doesn't recognize him. But you know him, because he lives with you now and later will be in you. (John 14:15-17 - NLT).

The Spirit's infilling is the personal manifestation of Christ in the life of the believer as he walks daily according to

God's Word. The believer must be forever conscious of this ongoing experience. Whereas every believer has the Holy Spirit, the filling is not automatic but is dependent on knowing and walking in obedience to the Word, while acknowledging the nudgings of the Holy Spirit. The infilling with the Holy Spirit requires obedience and submission on the believer's part, which is a major part of their responsibility. It is not up to the believer to endeavour to manufacture the results through effort but rather to yield to the Spirit's influence.

"Filled" is from the Greek word "plero" and has a number of applications contextually:

1. **Pressure** – Speaks to the wind billowing a ship's sails and providing the impetus for it to move forward across the waters. The believer is thereby provided with the thrust to help them move down the pathway of obedience. The Spirit-filled believer is not moved or motivated by their own desires or will but by the dictates of the Spirit. Another applicable imagery is that of a stick in a stream being carried by the force of the water. Thus, the Spirit will move or inspire a believer into correctness of action. Being filled is not just the utterance of language but the Spirit's personal presence transforming the lives of believers. In many instances, the Spirit will provide supernatural ability to function.

2. **Permeation** – This speaks to the Spirit permeating the life of the believer, imparting the very life of the Holy Spirit. This is akin to the effervescent effects of tablets releasing bubbles, colour and flavour to water. The believer, therefore, takes on the character of the Holy Spirit and produces the fruit thereof. This influence is infectious and easily identifiable and acknowledges the source.

3. **Domination** – This speaks to total control; to be dominated by a particular emotion or be fully exercised by the influence of another. This will affect the believer's thoughts, seeking to exclude every other emotion. The believer, however, must yield or surrender to the total control of the Spirit. Thus, the believer becomes more compliant and in submission to God's will, which is to their benefit. Being dominated by the Spirit means coming under the control of the Word and obeying the truth.

*And let the peace that comes from Christ rule in your hearts. For as members of one body you are called to live in peace. And always be thankful. Let the message about Christ, in all its richness, fill your lives. Teach and counsel each other with all the wisdom he gives. Sing psalms and hymns and spiritual songs to God with thankful hearts. (Colossians 3:15-16 - NLT)***.**

THREE EVIDENCE OR TRAITS OF A SPIRIT-FILLED LIFE

1. ***Has A Singing Spirit*** – This is a remarkable consequence of being Spirit-filled; the ascendency of worship in song. This contrasts with the singing of a drunk under the influence of alcohol. It is a picture of sheer joy and happiness as the believer expresses their experience of having the fullness of the Spirit. It is the Spirit that will prompt this joyous outburst.

2. **Has A Thankful Spirit** – Remains steadfast in their thankfulness to God in all things and for all things. There is the understanding that God is absolutely in control and sovereign. Being thankful is often a prerequisite to experiencing the fullness of the Spirit. The Spirit will help us to display an attitude of gratitude always.

   Always be full of joy in the Lord. I say it again—rejoice! Let everyone see that you are considerate in all you do. Remember, the Lord is coming soon. Don't worry about anything; instead, pray about everything. Tell God what you need, and thank him for all he has done. Then you will experience God's peace, which exceeds anything we can understand. His peace will guard your hearts and minds as you live in Christ Jesus. (Philippians 4:4-7 - NLT).

Give thanks to the LORD and proclaim his greatness. Let the whole world know what he has done. Sing to him; yes, sing his praises. Tell everyone about his wonderful deeds. Exult in his holy name; rejoice, you who worship the LORD. (1 Chronicles 16:8-10 - NLT).

Thankfulness needs to become habitual even in the midst of difficulties.

3. ***Has A Submissive And Respectful Spirit*** – This is not a spirit of criticism, dissension, divisiveness, or selfishness. There is a total surrender to God and His authority. The believer becomes willing to serve and minister to others; places the needs of others above self. The believer possesses a high level of humility and is meek in their approach and interactions with others.

   Don't be selfish; don't try to impress others. Be humble, thinking of others as better than yourselves. Don't look out only for your own interests, but take an interest in others, too. (Philippians 2:3-4 - NLT).

   Obey your spiritual leaders, and do what they say. Their work is to watch over your souls, and they are accountable to God. Give them reason to do this with joy and not with sorrow. That would certainly not be for your benefit. (Hebrews 13:17 - NLT).

> *In the same way, you who are younger must accept the authority of the elders. And all of you, dress yourselves in humility as you relate to one another, for "God opposes the proud but gives grace to the humble." (1 Peter 5:5 - NLT).*

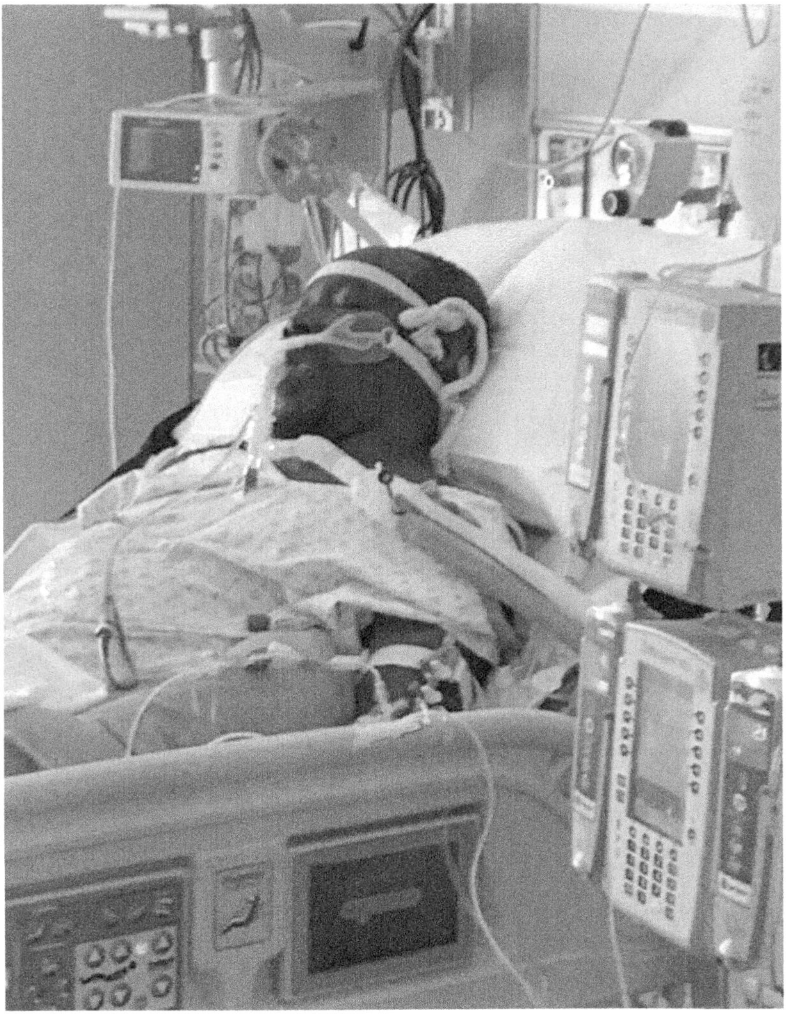

Hooked up to the ventilator in the ICU.

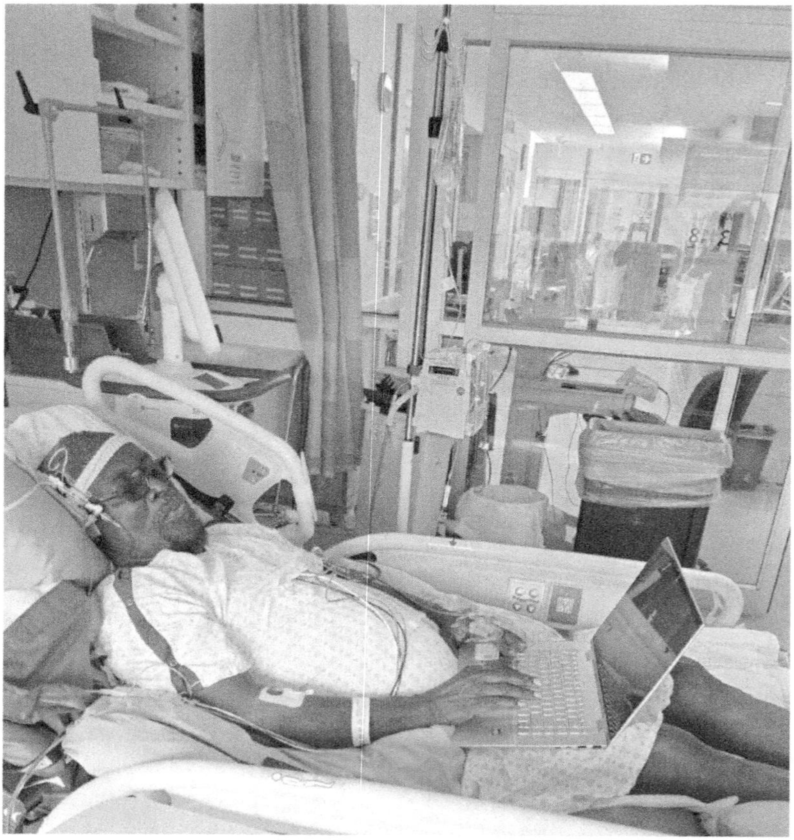

Working on the book "Giving Up Is Not An Option."

Discharged from the hospital (D-day).

Trying a thing.

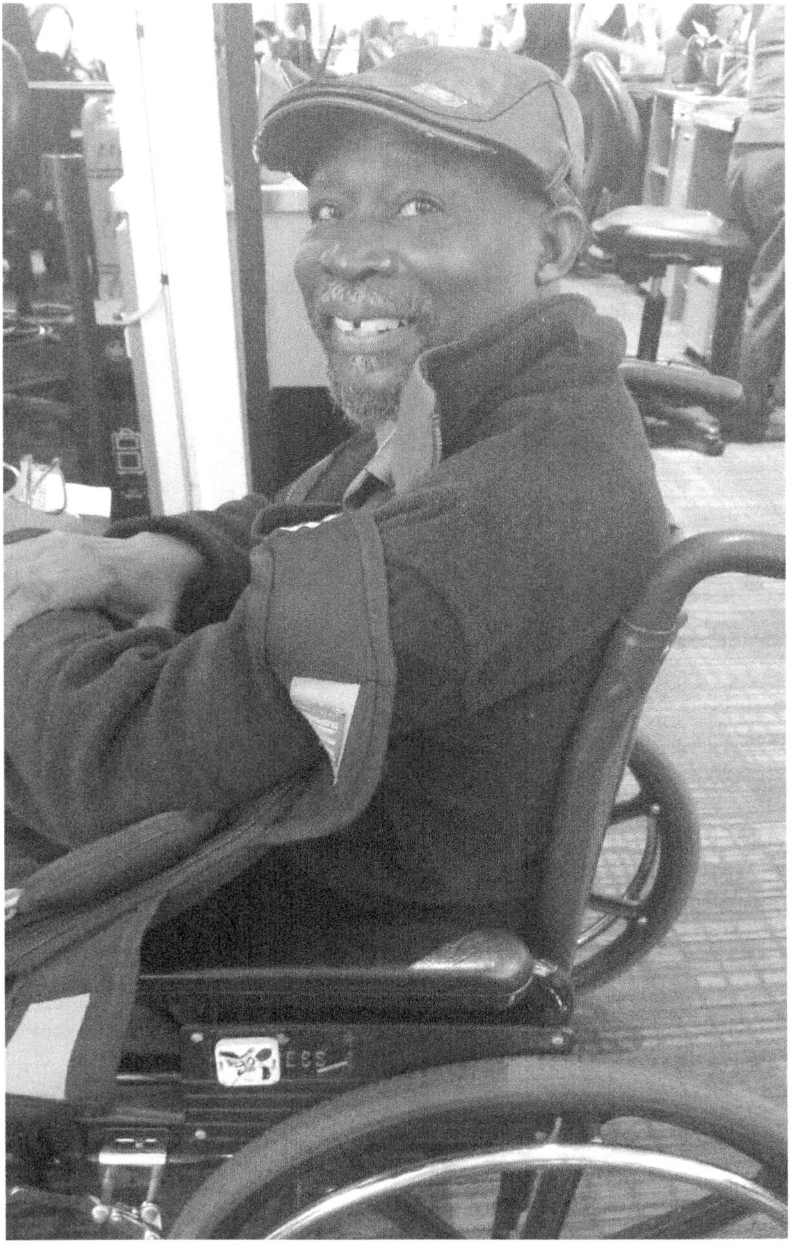
Wheelchair assistance for flight heading back to Jamaica.

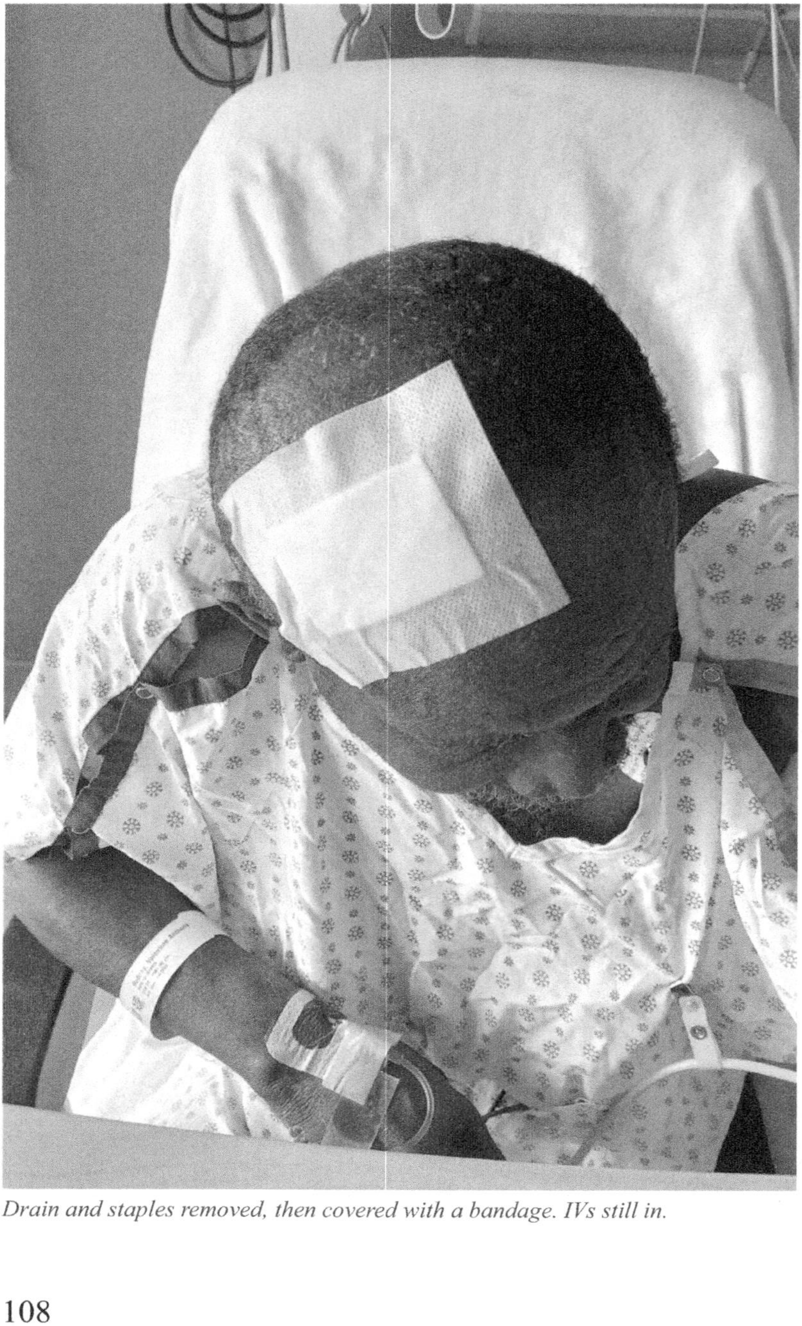

Drain and staples removed, then covered with a bandage. IVs still in.

My wife, Yevett (seated), along with Pastor Sophia Martin at the Women of Excellence Conference in Canada.

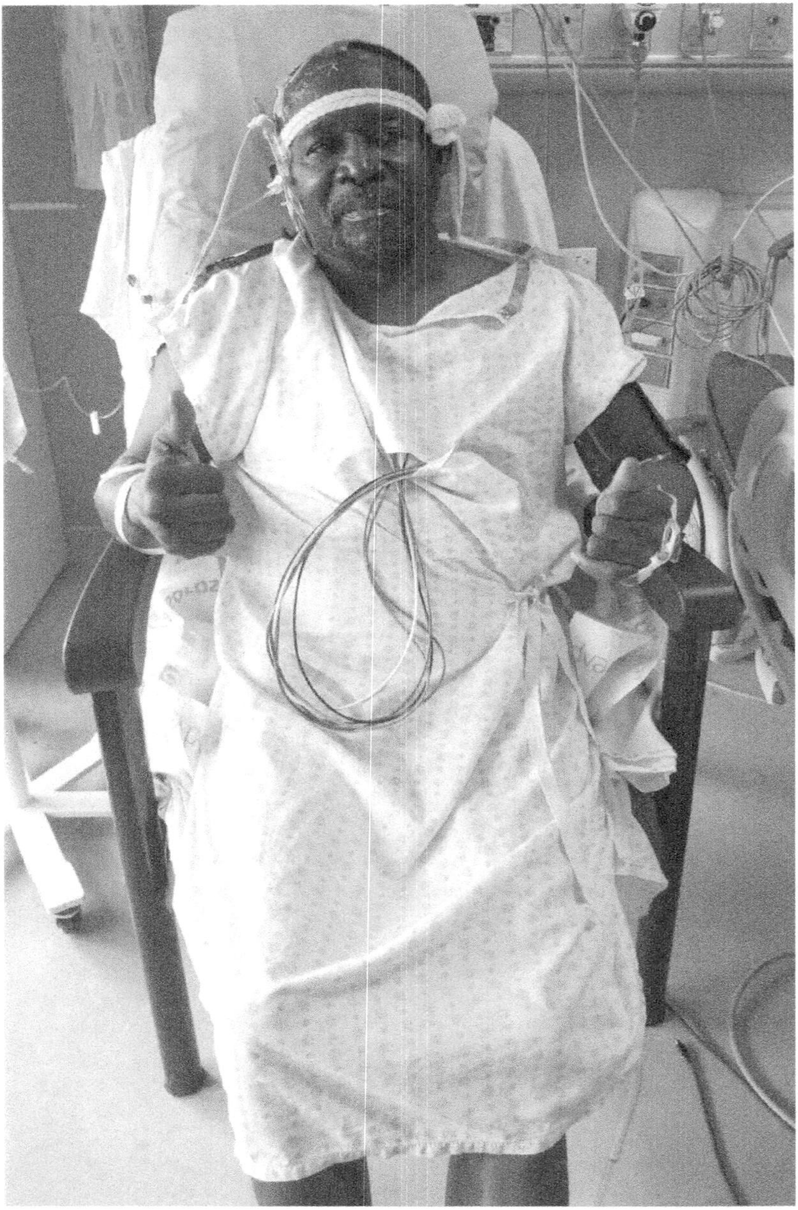

Seated in the ICU.

Thanks for the visit post-op Janice.

CHAPTER 9

THE EVIDENCE

But the believers who were scattered preached the Good News about Jesus wherever they went. Philip, for example, went to the city of Samaria and told the people there about the Messiah. Crowds listened intently to Philip because they were eager to hear his message and see the miraculous signs he did. Many evil spirits were cast out, screaming as they left their victims. And many who had been paralyzed or lame were healed. So there was great joy in that city. (Acts 8:4-8 - NLT).

The exploits of the people of God were manifested in the signs and wonders that accompanied the ministry of the Word of God. It is evident that miraculous signs were not limited to the apostles but accompanied the believers who preached the word in all the communities they went to because of the persecutions they faced. There was a strong and unwavering belief by all that God would show up and show forth wherever they went.

Two things attested and witnessed to the credibility of Philip's ministry. These were the message and the miraculous signs that accompanied it. The crowds heard the message but saw the miraculous signs that authenticated the message of Jesus that he brought. Philip was both fearless and faithful in his declaration. He both believed and proclaimed the message. The confirmation of the Word was the responsibility of the Holy Spirit. Philip's job was to faithfully preach the message concerning Jesus Christ, the Messiah.

True to the commission that Jesus had given to the apostles and, by extension, all believers, signs accompanied the Word. They did not preach for signs; they simply preached to make Jesus known. The signs put Jesus on display and confirmed the authenticity of the ministry. The conversions came because they were convicted in their hearts concerning the deity of the Lord Jesus Christ.

And then he told them, "Go into all the world and preach the Good News to everyone. Anyone who believes and is baptized will be saved. But anyone who refuses to believe will be condemned. These miraculous signs will accompany those who believe: They will cast out demons in my name, and they will speak in new languages. They will be able to handle snakes with safety, and if they drink anything poisonous, it won't hurt them. They will be able to place their hands on the sick, and they will be healed." (Mark 16:15-18 - NLT).

Philip was very conscious that he was on a mission with Christ and expected Christ to endorse the ministry. The signs simply pointed to Jesus and not the apostle. Those converted were not won to Philip but to Christ. Jesus pointed out in the Great Commission that the expulsion of demons was an integral identifier of God at work in the life of the believer. In fact, His providential care and protection were guaranteed as they went about their assignment.

"The Spirit of the LORD is upon me, for he has anointed me to bring Good News to the poor. He has sent me to proclaim that captives will be released, that the blind will see, that the oppressed will be set free, and that the time of the LORD's favor has come." (Luke 4:18-19 - NLT).

The message and ministry of Christ were abundantly clear and involved the deliverance of those who had been oppressed or victimized by the adversary. Jesus' ministry was one of saving from the clutches of disastrous situations. The cycles of oppression could not stand in the way of His sovereignty.

Look, I have given you authority over all the power of the enemy, and you can walk among snakes and scorpions and crush them. Nothing will injure you. (Luke 10:19 - NLT).

Jesus authorized the disciples as He sent them forth to accomplish the Kingdom's initiative that no evil force would be able to stop them. They saw visible displays of demonic subjugation because of this authority. It was clear that the preaching of the gospel would often result in power encounters. This would be the resistance encountered as territory was taken and brought under the Lordship of Jesus Christ. The believer already has God's backing and approval, which will undoubtedly facilitate divine displacement.

The believer, therefore, can traverse this planet with confidence, knowing that God has not abdicated His responsibility. Wherever we show up, He is already there to fulfill His Word.

The ministry of Christ within the life of the believer will be evidenced by miraculous signs that will attest to both the sovereignty and the workings of God. It is to be clearly noted that the Lord confirmed the preaching of the Word with miraculous signs that authenticated Him at work and clearly put Him on display. Jesus' mission on earth did not end at the crucifixion but continued in earnest post-resurrection through His disciples. This charge was given to the disciples post-resurrection and emphasizes that the continuation of the ministry of Jesus would be evident by the working of the Holy Spirit in the lives of the believers, just as Jesus had promised.

The signs and miracles were intended to draw people to Jesus and not to show or display the greatness of the disciples. The supernatural displays that accompanied the gospel message were for impactful witness. It validated and lent credence to the message. The gospel is a message that demonstrates God's power and authority to disrupt human agendas and avail Himself to all who will believe.

For I am not ashamed of this Good News about Christ. It is the power of God at work, saving everyone who believes—the Jew first and also the Gentile. This Good News tells us how God makes us right in his sight. This is accomplished from start to finish by faith. As the Scriptures say, "It is through faith that a righteous person has life." (Romans 1:16-17 - NLT).

FRUITFULNESS – THE EVIDENCE OF ABIDING IN CHRIST

"I am the true grapevine, and my Father is the gardener. He cuts off every branch of mine that doesn't produce fruit, and he prunes the branches that do bear fruit so they will produce even more. You have already been pruned and purified by the message I have given you. Remain in me, and I will remain in you. For a branch cannot produce fruit if it is severed from the vine, and you cannot be fruitful unless you remain in me. "Yes, I am the vine; you are the branches. Those who remain in me, and I in them, will produce much fruit. For apart from me you can do nothing. Anyone who does not remain in me is thrown away like a useless branch and withers. Such branches are gathered into a pile to be burned. But if you remain in me and my words remain in you, you may ask for anything you want, and it will be granted! When you produce much fruit, you are my true

disciples. This brings great glory to my Father. (John 15:1-8 - NLT).

There is a direct correlation between fruit and the type of tree, fruitfulness, and the branch to which it is connected. This concept was not lost on the people of the day who lived in basically an agrarian society. Jesus would use His teachings and experiences drawn from everyday life, which would cause His teachings to come alive and the applications to be understandable. The practical nature of His teachings used the familiar to explain the unfamiliar.

Jesus distinguishes Himself from Israel as God's vine to Himself as the true vine. Thus, we must be rooted in Him and not Israel or the church. In this concept, the emphasis is on complete trust and dependence as we maintain our connectivity with Christ. The importance of this connectivity cannot be underscored, and it is indeed far greater than any other human relationship. The union provides support alongside all we need to be complete in Him. What He is will manifest through us.

The believer must have an integral relationship with Father and Son or Vinedresser and Vine. This is the established pattern of existence that is referred to. There can be no relationship with the Father and not with the Son and also vice versa. There is a level of interconnectedness that is explicitly stated.

The true evidence of being connected to Christ or abiding in the Vine is symbolized in fruit-bearing. Fruit is a visible sign of one's relationship with Christ. A tree is truly known by the fruit that it bears. Fruit does not err. Who you are connected to will determine what you produce. The very character of Christ will be displayed by those who are truly connected to Him. Fruitfulness is the hallmark of abiding.

In the original construct of creation, every tree followed the order of producing after its own kind. It should, therefore, be natural for the believer to produce the fruit of the Spirit based on their abiding relationship with Christ and complete surrender to the Holy Spirit.

But the Holy Spirit produces this kind of fruit in our lives: love, joy, peace, patience, kindness, goodness, faithfulness, gentleness, and self-control. There is no law against these things! (Galatians 5:22-23 - NLT).

Then God said, "Let the land sprout with vegetation—every sort of seed-bearing plant, and trees that grow seed-bearing fruit. These seeds will then produce the kinds of plants and trees from which they came." And that is what happened. (Genesis 1:11 - NLT).

This was basically a law instituted from the dawn of creation that a seed would only produce after its own kind, the plant from which it came. You can, therefore, undeniably name a tree based on its fruit. The fruit is also evidence of the productivity of a tree—evidence that a new cycle has begun and that the possibility of continuation exists.

"Beware of false prophets who come disguised as harmless sheep but are really vicious wolves. You can identify them by their fruit, that is, by the way they act. Can you pick grapes from thornbushes, or figs from thistles? A good tree produces good fruit, and a bad tree produces bad fruit. A good tree can't produce bad fruit, and a bad tree can't produce good fruit. So every tree that does not produce good fruit is chopped down and thrown into the fire. Yes, just as you can identify a tree by its fruit, so you can identify people by their actions. (Matthew 7:15-20 - NLT).

The indwelling presence of the Holy Spirit will produce fruit in the lives of the believers. There will be visible evidence and ongoing manifestations of the Holy Spirit's presence that will influence the character formation of the individual.

The Father is the Vine Dresser, and the Son is the True Vine. It is important to note that the believer has an intimate relationship with both the Father and Son. The branch (believer) depends on the Vine for support and nutrition. The branch cannot exist or fulfill its purpose if separated from the Vine. There is, therefore, the need for constant connectivity.

The true evidence of abiding is fruitfulness. Anything unfruitful is taken away. The idea of "taken away" could mean pruning to become more fruitful or to lift from off the ground to provide an advantage to secure fruit bearing.

"Better to be pruned to grow than cut up to burn."

—Trapp.

The Vinedresser is responsible for cleaning up the branches so they can become more fruitful.

Prayer becomes spontaneous to those who are connected to and abiding in Christ. It becomes so much easier to submit and pray His will from that deep-seated sense of communion and intimacy. For the believer, the Word of God becomes an integral part of their make up. You can't believe in Jesus and not embrace His Word.

CHAPTER 10

PRISON BREAK

God's resources are infinitely bigger than our expectations. That is what makes Him dependable and reliable. God sees the end before we experience the heat of the conflict. The infant church was now facing increased hostility from the powers that be.

There was a succession of Herod's that came to power, and their reign was each marked by persecution in one form or the other. The rise in the persecution of the church by King Herod Agrippa did not shut down the witness of the church. They stood their ground amid adversity and continued to trust God either for deliverance or grace.

It is up to God and His sovereignty to decide whether He will deliver us from a challenging situation or provide the grace to sustain us. Herod's initial assault on the community of believers ended with both the capture and execution of James. Deliverance is not based on worthiness but on sovereignty and purpose. Trusting in God is not manipulation or coercion but submission to His will. He has the final say in all matters of faith and prayer.

The church did not wilt because of the casualty and ensuing pressures but rather became militant in their advocacy upon the subsequent capture of Peter with the intent of killing him also.

Then he imprisoned him, placing him under the guard of four squads of four soldiers each. Herod intended to bring Peter out for public trial after the Passover. But while Peter was in prison, the church prayed very earnestly for him. (Acts 12:4-5 - NLT).

This was corporate intercession at its best. This was not directing God in His decision-making but asking for a favourable outcome to the crisis. It was a continuous (unceasing) prayer that was offered by the entire church community on behalf of Peter. It was God's will to respond to this call for intervention on Peter's behalf. While the church was up praying, Peter was asleep in prison, chained between soldiers. Prayer must reveal God's will rather than reinforce our desires.

And we are confident that he hears us whenever we ask for anything that pleases him. And since we know he hears us when we make our requests, we also know that he will give us what we ask for. (1 John 5:14-15 - NLT).

The scriptures are clear that answered prayers are based on what pleases God, which is consistent with His will. God is more concerned about His will than our comfort. Rest assured that it was not who Peter was why he escaped being a casualty but rather who God is.

Powerful and effective prayers are based more on the God who responds than the nature of us who are praying.

Therefore, confess your sins to one another [your false steps, your offenses], and pray for one another, that you may be healed and restored. The heartfelt and persistent prayer of a righteous man (believer) can accomplish much [when put into action and made effective by God—it is dynamic and can have tremendous power]. (James 5:16 - AMP).

The power and effectiveness of the believer's prayer is based wholly on the God who answers. Evidently, the huddled believing church were privy to and praying according to divine intelligence. It is impossible to pray amiss or selfishly when the Holy Spirit is guiding you to pray for a specific outcome.

Prayer must be deemed a necessary pre-requisite for engaging the sovereign God in a supernatural way. They were confident of not only being heard but responded to affirmatively. Engaging God in prayer must make us privy to revelation that brings an understanding of what He desires to accomplish. Through revelation, we are not only expectant but confident about the outcome. This will generate both passion and commitment to be earnest in prayer and committed to action. Great confidence and trust are embodied in praying according to God's will.

God responded to the prayers of the saints by facilitating an extraordinary prison break for Peter. This was done on the eve of Herod's decision to subject Peter to the same fate as James. The prison became subject to a supernatural invasion by an angel with the sole purpose or intent being to deliver Peter. This was done effortlessly and without raising an alarm. Despite being guarded by sixteen soldiers, the miraculous deliverance was wrought without a hitch. The captors were unaware of the prisoner's exit.

This was clearly evidence of God's supernatural power at work. The security system of Herod was no match for God's Divine intervention. The soldiers were unaware of the angelic visitor, the light in the prison, Peter dressing in preparation to leave, and the chains to the guards falling off. God facilitated Peter's rescue without the aid of human involvement. This was not flesh and blood at work but a supernatural display of God's working power.

The supernatural visitor guided Peter, who thought he was seeing a vision, through the various guard stations until they reached the iron gate that led to the city. This gate miraculously opened to them by itself without being manipulated by anyone.

Recognising that he had escaped from the prison and navigated through the streets, he acknowledged God's role in his deliverance. He had been saved from Herod's intended punishment and all the schemes the Jewish leaders devised.

Peter finally came to his senses. "It's really true!" he said. "The Lord has sent his angel and saved me from Herod and from what the Jewish leaders had planned to do to me!" (Acts 12:11 (- NLT).

On Peter's arrival at the house of Mary, the mother of John, he found that many had gathered and were engaged in intense prayer and travail for him.

CHAPTER 11

WALKING IN LOVE

So now I am giving you a new commandment: Love each other. Just as I have loved you, you should love each other. Your love for one another will prove to the world that you are my disciples." (John 13:34-35 - NLT).

One of the major hallmarks of being a disciple hinges on a demonstration of love. This is not theoretical but practical in its demonstration. We must love in word and deed.

Therefore become imitators of God [copy Him and follow His example], as well-beloved children [imitate their father]; and walk continually in love [that is, value one another—practice empathy and compassion, unselfishly seeking the best for others], just as Christ also loved you and gave Himself up for us, an offering and sacrifice to God [slain for you, so that it became] a sweet fragrance. (Ephesians 5:1-2 - AMP).

Imitation is an essential attribute of love as we seek to follow and model the example that is set before us. With a correct example, the evidence of love will be maximised in our behaviour as we seek to follow and learn from what we see and understand.

As God loves us, we love him, and we love others and, indeed, ourselves. We are called to be like God in this area of our lives. We care for and do not abuse who we love. Love is both the hallmark of discipleship and our relationship with God. God-like love will be manifested in us loving as liberally as He does.

Imitate:

- To imitate is to copy.
- To reproduce what you have seen and understood.
- To submit to God and not rebel.
- To demonstrate commitment, attachment, devotion, and attention to God as we follow.
- It involves total surrender and the devotion of your life to God.
- The process through which we follow and adhere to the righteous standards He has laid down.

The love of God is affirming and not belittling. He accepts and embraces us, despite who we are, because of the depth of His love for us. This is the behaviour we are expected to reciprocate based on what we have received. Love, by the nature of what it is, initiates a response.

Jesus silenced the Sadducees who were testing Him with the question concerning which is the greatest commandment. He specified the love of God and neighbour, not just who you choose but those you might not even consider. You can't love God (vertical) and not love man (horizontal). Both are inextricably linked to each other.

"Teacher, which is the most important commandment in the law of Moses?" Jesus replied, "'You must love the LORD your God with all your heart, all your soul, and all your mind.' This is the first and greatest commandment. A second is equally important: 'Love your neighbor as yourself.' The entire law and all the demands of the prophets are based on these two commandments." (Matthew 22:36-40 - NLT).

For love to be identified, it must have an outlet or a means of expression. You know love best by the characteristics it exhibits. This implies dealing with others without partiality or preferences and assisting those in need, even if they are from different ethnic persuasions. In fact, the parable suggested that the one who loved his neighbour was the one who showed mercy. We cannot have the resources and not offer help, yet claim to have the love of God.

If someone has enough money to live well and sees a brother or sister in need but shows no compassion—how can God's love be in that person? Dear children, let's not merely say that we love each other; let us show the truth by our actions. (1 John 3:17-18 - NLT).

Jesus emphasises that love is not optional; it is a biblical imperative. In fact, our relationship with God is demonstrated in our love for others. Followers of Christ would exemplify the theme of love. When we love each other, we always seek the best.

So now I am giving you a new commandment: Love each other. Just as I have loved you, you should love each other. Your love for one another will prove to the world that you are my disciples." (John 13:34-35 - NLT).

Dear friends, let us continue to love one another, for love comes from God. Anyone who loves is a child of God and knows God. (1 John 4:7 - NLT).

Love is generally self-sacrificing. The caring commitment shows itself by seeking the highest good of the one loved.

CHARACTERISTICS OF GOD'S LOVE THAT MUST BE EVIDENT IN US

- **God's love is costly.** He gave His own Son, who was willing to lay down His life for us. We must also lay aside selfishness and self-centredness as we serve each other. We must get over our pride and rights.

- **God's love is caring.** There must be a show of compassion where we care deeply and are compassionate of others.

- **God's love is committed.** He went to the cross not because it felt good, but He was committed to saving His people from their sins. Commitment is the glue that makes love endure.

- **God's love is conspicuous.** It shows itself clearly, not just in thoughts but deeds; not just what you say but what you do.

- **God's love is a consecrating love.** It seeks the highest good of the one loved. There is tremendous dedication to the cause.

  He did this to present her to himself as a glorious church without a spot or wrinkle or any other blemish. Instead, she will be holy and without fault. (Ephesians 5:27 - NLT).

"Consecrating" implies correcting and imposing consequences for wrong behaviour. It may require being confrontational regarding behaviour. Where there is no correction, the love is shallow.

Don't just pretend to love others. Really love them. Hate what is wrong. Hold tightly to what is good. (Romans 12:9 - NLT).

Walking in love is a lifelong process. The process involves slow, steady, and deliberate steps. This must be done with all humility and gentleness, with patience, and showing tolerance for one another in love. Interpersonal communications require speaking the truth in love and growing together in love as the body ministers to itself. Incorruptible love for Jesus Christ is the standard for all believers.

The longer you are a committed Christian, the more your life should be characterised by love.

But we don't need to write to you about the importance of loving each other, for God himself has taught you to love one another. Indeed, you already show your love for all the believers throughout Macedonia. Even so, dear brothers and sisters, we urge you to love them even more. (1 Thessalonians 4:9-10 - NLT).

We are taught by God to love the brethren even though that will come with its fair share of challenges. It is not optional or left up to our discretion but an imperative that we love as He loved. God not only teaches us how to, but He, through the Holy Spirit, gives us the capacity to love impartially.

HOW DID CHRIST LOVE PEOPLE?

He was kind and gentle with the broken but forceful and direct with the proud and hypocritical. He lovingly corrected and embraced. Sacrificial love was always at the forefront and was His primary motivation. He loved the unloved and the despised and treated them honourably. In loving others, we seek to glorify and reverence God, not necessarily seek a reciprocal response from others. Do not wait to be shown love; rather, show love to all, whether it is returned or not.

Love is hard to define but easy to identify by its characteristics. Love is clear evidence that we are in relationship with the Lord Jesus Christ. The behaviour outlined in the text below clearly demonstrates what we should possess and demonstrate to all. It is both precept and example. These must be evident in all levels of interpersonal relationships:

Love is patient and kind. Love is not jealous or boastful or proud or rude. It does not demand its own way. It is not irritable, and it keeps no record of being wronged. It does not rejoice about injustice but rejoices whenever the truth wins out. Love never gives up, never loses faith, is always hopeful, and endures through every circumstance. (1 Corinthians 13:4-7 - NLT).

All the believers devoted themselves to the apostles' teaching, and to fellowship, and to sharing in meals (including the Lord's Supper), and to prayer. A deep sense of awe came over them all, and the apostles performed many miraculous signs and wonders. And all the believers met together in one place and shared everything they had. They sold their property and possessions and shared the money with those in need. They worshiped together at the Temple each day, met in homes for the Lord's Supper, and shared their meals with great joy and generosity—all the while praising God and enjoying the goodwill of all the people.

And each day the Lord added to their fellowship those who were being saved. (Acts 2:42-47 - NLT).

The infant church demonstrated one of the most practical acts and demonstrations of Christianity, which had to do with fellowship. This is the glue that holds believers together in community. They demonstrated this without partiality in addressing administrative oversight. It is clear that the same care must be exhibited one for another.

Your love for one another will prove to the world that you are my disciples." (John 13:35 - NLT).

Even though Jesus made the disciples aware of the supernatural signs that would accompany ministry, He was quick to establish that the real hallmark or evidence of discipleship is love.

CHAPTER 12

LIVING BEYOND LIMITS

And Jabez was more honourable than his brethren: and his mother called his name Jabez, saying, Because I bare him with sorrow. And Jabez called on the God of Israel, saying, Oh that thou wouldest bless me indeed, and enlarge my coast, and that thine hand might be with me, and that thou wouldest keep me from evil, that it may not grieve me! And God granted him that which he requested. (1 Chronicles 4:9-10 - KJV).

There was a man named Jabez who was more honorable than any of his brothers. His mother named him Jabez because his birth had been so painful. He was the one who prayed to the God of Israel, "Oh, that you would bless me and expand my territory! Please be with me in all that I do, and keep me from all trouble and pain!" And God granted him his request. (1 Chronicles 4:9-10 - NLT).

God's plan is always bigger than your pain. The beginning of a thing does not necessarily mean the end of the matter. The inevitability of change often indicates that a bad beginning does not necessarily imply a bad ending. A positive life can emerge from an extremely bad or challenging start.

There are so many variables to life that will often make things appear unpredictable. There are many things that could not have been prevented; however, the display of God's power can cause intervention. We must always remember that despite great odds, we serve a great God.

The life of Jabez is indeed a case study that demonstrates that you can start with negativity but still have a positive outcome because of God's involvement and intervention in your life. The narrative is going to describe that though things started bad, he prayed and committed both the circumstances and his life to God, and it all ended well. You have reached a point in your life where things are about to pivot a full 180 degrees.

The prayer is going to reflect four basic components.

1. Jabez asked God to bless him.
2. He asked God to enlarge his territory or increase his sphere of responsibility.
3. He prayed that God would be with him and stay close to him.
4. He asked that God would keep him from harm so he would be free from pain.

It is never where you begin but the journey you take and where you ultimately end up. The story of Jabez reveals that things started very badly for him, but he prayed to God and experienced a turnaround. He was unwilling to accept the current status quo and was convinced that God could bring about the desired change. Unless your philosophy or belief system changes, your behaviour will not follow suit. When you change, things around you will respond. In the words of John Edmond Haggai, "Attempt something so great for God that it is doomed for failure unless God be with it."

You can exceed expectations and not be restricted by the previous achievements of others. One thing you can exercise mastery over is yourself. This speaks to not being intimidated or overshadowed by the achievements of others or being plagued and accepting of life's fears and insecurities.

The name Jabez means "sorrow maker" and is associated with pain and discomfort. It is thought that he received the name because of the harshness of the time surrounding his birth or due to his mother having an extremely difficult pregnancy. He made a conscious decision that the name he bore would not become his destiny in life. Sometimes, it is not what you are called but what you respond to and are convicted of.

ASK GOD TO BLESS YOU

It is important to be resolute in your desire for change and have the conviction and confidence that a positive change is inevitable. It is important to recognise that Jabez sought divine intervention to deal with the magnitude of this situation. The laws of limitation must not apply, and we must remember that a bad start does not equate to a bad ending. You must be brave enough to both confront and conquer your challenges. It is in working on yourself that the positive benefits will accrue. I trust that you will reach the point of realisation that trusting in God will produce worthwhile changes but requires the application of His Word. With resolve, you must finish what you started. A change in behaviour will require a change in belief.

There are some aspects of change that require divine intervention and others that are a product of our own will and conviction. So, like Jabez, ask God to bless you. We should not complain about receiving if we never ask. You must never embrace any unwritten rules that you will never succeed in life. Whatever the limitations, the barriers must be broken. Like Jabez, we need to ask for supernatural favour and God's unlimited goodness in our lives. May God grant to us what is best for our lives.

Jabez acknowledged the importance of God's role in his life but left it up to God to determine the way He would choose to bless him. It was God's expectation that was deemed most important. Everything that was not geared to becoming a blessing must be canceled, and everything godly must be deployed to work for good on His behalf and in keeping with God's divine will. There must be the realisation that to secure a blessed future, we depend on God to orchestrate it all. We secure our future by the decisions we make and the life we live today.

ASK GOD TO ENLARGE YOUR SPHERE OF INFLUENCE

Our asking must be in accordance with an understanding of our God-ordained destiny. Jabez wanted an increase in impact and opportunities to succeed. What has God entrusted to us that we have not yet accessed? May God displace all ungodly influences and bring the kind of order to our lives that will prepare us for unlimited success. With an increase in impact comes increased responsibility.

THAT GOD'S HAND WOULD BE UPON HIM

He was asking for God's providential care and divine guidance in all aspects of his life. Implicit in this request is a desire for personal protection and safety.

KEEP HIM FROM EVIL

Success brings with it great opportunities for failure. Success requires an invasion of enemy territory to establish and exercise dominion.

The evidence that Jabez's prayer was heard is that God granted his request.

CHAPTER 13

WORKING THE WORKS OF GOD

As Jesus was walking along, he saw a man who had been blind from birth. "Rabbi," his disciples asked him, "why was this man born blind? Was it because of his own sins or his parents' sins?" "It was not because of his sins or his parents' sins," Jesus answered. "This happened so the power of God could be seen in him. We must quickly carry out the tasks assigned us by the one who sent us. The night is coming, and then no one can work. (John 9:1-4 - NLT).

Limits can be self-imposed or a consequence of the actions of another. The man at the center of this miraculous display of God's power had a problem that was literally considered to be incurable. The man's condition was congenital. He was born with an inability to see. This physical defect not only posed significant challenges but also affected popular perception. The disciples voiced these sentiments as they echoed the popular belief of the day that being born blind was attributed to either sin by the unborn child or parental figures. The thought is not readily embraced that God can allow challenges to effect change. Suffering and hardship can be part of God's plan to provide deliverance and put Himself on display.

Not only was the man born blind but it was now being used to gain financial support through their extension of sympathy. The disciples must have been aware of his story based on the man's own proclamation, hence the nature of their question.

They were more interested in centering their discussions about the man's challenges than helping him. Jesus was more concerned with the man's healing than any theological considerations regarding his condition. Charles Spurgeon reminds us that "It is ours, not to speculate, but to perform acts of mercy and love, according to the tenor of the gospel. Let us then be less inquisitive and more practical, less for cracking doctrinal nuts, and more for bringing forth the bread of life to the starving multitudes."

People normally associate unusual sufferings with unusual sins. The disciples saw this as an act of divine retribution being heaped upon this man. There was no feeling of sympathy or extension of compassion because of their perception. Consider the prevailing thought of the time: "There is no death without sin, and there is no suffering without iniquity."

Dods suggested five possible reasons behind the disciple's question:

1. Some of the Jews of that time believed in the pre-existence of souls, and the possibility that those pre-existent souls could sin.

2. Some of the Jews at that time believed in some kind of reincarnation, and perhaps the man sinned in a previous existence.

3. Some of the Jews at that time believed that a baby might sin in the womb.

4. They thought the punishment was for a sin the man would later commit.

5. They were so bewildered that they threw out a wild possibility without thinking it through.

Jesus held the view that no specific sin had contributed to the man's condition or demise, which was contrary to popular viewpoint. Many maladies have come to the earth because of man's original sin. Jesus, much to their surprise, indicated that the man's blindness was a part of God's plan. Jesus' emphasis was not on why but more so that God could and would alleviate his suffering—no prevention but intervention based on God's sovereignty.

For the scripture saith unto Pharaoh, Even for this same purpose have I raised thee up, that I might shew my power in thee, and that my name might be declared throughout all the earth. (Romans 9:17 - KJV).

The evidence of God working in human history was to be manifested in this man's healing.

"Evil furthers the work of God in the world. It is in conquering and abolishing evil that He is manifested. The question for us is not where suffering has come from, but what are we to do with it."

—Dods

Jesus indicated that whatever caused the blindness was going to be overruled by God, resulting in a restoration of sight. This negative situation was going to be used to further God's agenda in creating a platform for belief in Him. It was more about God's sovereignty rather than evil's supremacy. God has the antidote for a wide array of human sufferings and maladies. He can usurp the authority that any of them can impose on humanity and visibly provide evidence of healing and deliverance.

Jesus saw the man's condition as an opportunity to display the works of God with a sense of urgency in dismissing what had held him in bondage from birth. What appeared to be a challenge and nigh unto impossible with man was well within God's omnipotence.

Dealing with the man's suffering was going to put Jesus on display. Despite it being the sabbath, His compassion drove Him to execute this healing. Location and time cannot hinder the performance of God. He is capable of changing misfortune to fortune.

Jesus was never restricted to performing healings the same way each time. He could either use a word, a touch, or the application of physical materials with some basic instructions. In this case, He used spittle mixed with clay to place on the man's eyes, and then He instructed him to go wash in the pool of Siloam. Using saliva as a medicine upon the eyes was not so strange in the ancient world.

"Spittle, and especially the spittle of some distinguished persons, was believed to possess certain curative qualities."
—Barclay

"The virtue of the fasting saliva, in the cases of disorders of the eye, was well known to antiquity."
—Alford

Mark recorded two other healings that Jesus performed with the use of His saliva (see Mark 7:33 and 8:23).

The miracle was executed as he moved in obedience to the Word of God. This took faith and confidence in submitting to the instructions of Jesus. He had to believe and obey for the evidence of his compliance to manifest or come to fruition.

NOT DEAD BUT ASLEEP

While he was still speaking to her, messengers arrived from the home of Jairus, the leader of the synagogue. They told him, "Your daughter is dead. There's no use troubling the

Teacher now." But Jesus overheard them and said to Jairus, "Don't be afraid. Just have faith." Then Jesus stopped the crowd and wouldn't let anyone go with him except Peter, James, and John (the brother of James). When they came to the home of the synagogue leader, Jesus saw much commotion and weeping and wailing. He went inside and asked, "Why all this commotion and weeping? The child isn't dead; she's only asleep." The crowd laughed at him. But he made them all leave, and he took the girl's father and mother and his three disciples into the room where the girl was lying. Holding her hand, he said to her, "Talitha koum," which means "Little girl, get up!" And the girl, who was twelve years old, immediately stood up and walked around! They were overwhelmed and totally amazed. Jesus gave them strict orders not to tell anyone what had happened, and then he told them to give her something to eat. (Mark 5:35-43 - NLT).

The reputation of Jesus by now was well known, and many had seen or benefited from His power to heal. Jairus had a great desire to see evidence of this grace. He was a local synagogue official but was convinced that Jesus could provide a miraculous cure for his 12-year-old daughter's sickness. Some have assumed that she had succumbed to a diabetic coma.

Jairus knew that his status and position were not enough to effect the cure that was needed for his daughter. He demonstrated both humility and faith in seeking out assistance from Jesus. The need he had was greater than his embarrassment to ask. He was seeking a miracle from the Messiah and not a relationship. He did not entrust the seeking after Jesus to anyone else. He came himself to encourage Jesus to come to his house and heal his daughter.

Needs have a way of causing the seeker to display much humility. His posture was to ask Jesus, believing that Jesus could do it but hoping that He would. Despite the urgent nature of the request, he remained reverential and expectant. Within the sphere of his own family crisis or household problem, he needed a solution to what had thrown his whole world into a tailspin. One family member having an emergency can cause the entire family to be destabilized and feel threatened. The entire family can be stressed because of what one member is being subjected to.

Jairus was believing for healing, but Jesus was going to deliver a resurrection. Jesus will meet you at the point of your need. A crisis can either paralyze you through fear or propel you to a solution-seeking activity. The crisis created an opportunity for Jairus to demonstrate faith and adopt the posture of intercession as he pleaded with Christ on his daughter's behalf. Giving up was not an option to Jairus, and he shamelessly persevered. To obtain positive results from God requires us to trust Him and believe.

Seeking requires you to show up and allow your voice to be heard as you seek an answer to your existing situation. We must never allow our problems or fears to speak louder than our prayers and faith. The father was desperate and demanding and refused to be daunted. He had the conviction that there was still time despite his daughter being at the point of death. He would not fail her; Jesus simply had to come and lay His hands for her full and total recovery.

Jairus had made an informed decision to come to Jesus and firmly believed that Jesus Christ was his only hope. What he had heard, he must now know. Like those who had received testimonies and declared Jesus to be Messiah, he now needed evidence of same. He was convinced that this could not be an exercise in futility. He had made a full commitment and reached the point of no return.

Jesus was briefly interrupted on His journey to Jairus' house by the woman with the issue of blood. Much to the dismay of Jairus, the interruption was costly because news came from the house that his daughter was dead. The messengers, viewing the situation to be hopeless, implored Him to curtail His mission. We must endeavour to believe that in all matters where we are powerless, Jesus has the final say. Are you willing to believe that Jesus will uphold your appeal and grant a favourable verdict?

In the face of this new information, Jesus emphasized, "Don't be afraid, just believe, and she will be healed. The situation is not beyond the scope of My ability to help." Jairus could not have prevented her from dying but Jesus confirmed that He would intervene. Things had gotten worse, but Christ was about to make it better. The gravity of the problem does not in any way minimize the omnipotence of Christ. No matter how dire the circumstances are, we must never remove our trust from God.

Jairus was now privy to two sets of contrasting information and needed to decide. Remember, it is not just what you hear but what you respond to. Those from his house seemed to suggest that this was a failed venture and that the situation was hopeless. But the words of Christ were hopeful and encouraging. He had to overcome any sense of fear with faith. No matter how late the hour may seem, all is not lost. The mission will not end in failure or defeat. Sometimes what you see will not affect what will be.

The scene at Jairus's house was one of pandemonium where people were crying and wailing loudly, and the minstrels and people were making a noise, albeit in mourning. A cloud of hopelessness permeated the setting, but Christ remained unfazed.

He went inside and asked, "Why all this commotion and weeping? The child isn't dead; she's only asleep." The crowd laughed at him. But he made them all leave, and he took the girl's father and mother and his three disciples into the room where the girl was lying. (Mark 5:39-40 - NLT).

Jesus was not about to give a permanent endorsement to a temporary issue. His assessment did not agree with their observation. They had already accepted that it could never improve. But Jesus was adamant that there must be a visible display of divine power at work. Jesus inferred that there would be recovery.

The big question was, could Jesus back up His words? All those gathered were going to require more than just words; they wanted proof or evidence, and Jesus was not about to disappoint. The only evidence that would suffice is that of total and complete recovery of Jairus' daughter. The worldview that death was final was about to be shaken in all that had gathered. No matter how extreme your crisis is, God cannot fail and He will not fail you.

Jesus took her by the hand and told the child to get up, which she did, much to the amazement of those gathered. The miracle was immediate, and all functionalities were restored. The giving of something for her to eat clearly demonstrated that the miracle was complete. Feeding is one of the characteristics of the living and not the dead.

The girl carrying out her responsibilities was undeniable proof of a miracle. May the God you serve provide you with the evidence required to shut the mouth of the naysayers and affirm the faith and trust relationship of the believing community. Serving Christ is going to be proven to be evidence-based. Faith in God will produce the evidence.

Now all glory to God, who is able, through his mighty power at work within us, to accomplish infinitely more than we might ask or think. (Ephesians 3:20 - NLT).

CHAPTER 14

THROUGH THE FIRE

For our present troubles are small and won't last very long. Yet they produce for us a glory that vastly outweighs them and will last forever! So we don't look at the troubles we can see now; rather, we fix our gaze on things that cannot be seen. For the things we see now will soon be gone, but the things we cannot see will last forever. (2 Corinthians 4:17-18 - NLT).

So Satan left the LORD's presence, and he struck Job with terrible boils from head to foot. Job scraped his skin with a piece of broken pottery as he sat among the ashes. His wife said to him, "Are you still trying to maintain your integrity? Curse God and die." But Job replied, "You talk like a foolish woman. Should we accept only good things from the hand of God and never anything bad?" So in all this, Job said nothing wrong. (Job 2:7-10 - NLT).

We obtain a keen insight into the operations of the spiritual realm based on the interaction between God and the forces of evil. It must be understood that God is at work, even when He appears to be silent. Job was ignorant of the reason for the spate of challenges and difficulties he was experiencing but clung tenaciously to God in faith.

Sometimes, the evidence of our faith in God is manifested in standing and serving faithfully during the crisis. Job endured the testing of his faith initially through the loss of material things then family members. He might not have understood, but he was confident that God's purposes would prevail.

Not even the discouraging sentiments from His wife, which he sharply rebuked, could sway him from his commitment, considering that he was now suffering personally from boils. The only family member not slain by Satan was Job's wife, and this begs the question of whether she was spared to effect the purposes of Satan. Those who are ignorant of God's plan may be liable to doubt Him or speak against His works. God does provide good things; however, He is never absent when the negative arrives. He has the power to bring good out of a negative experience.

And we know that God causes everything to work together for the good of those who love God and are called according to his purpose for them. (Romans 8:28 - NLT).

The words of Satan in the dialogue are instructive and clearly demonstrate God's sovereignty in all situations.

Then the LORD asked Satan, "Have you noticed my servant Job? He is the finest man in all the earth. He is blameless—a man of complete integrity. He fears God and stays away from evil." Satan replied to the LORD, "Yes, but Job has good reason to fear God. You have always put a wall of protection around him and his home and his property. You have made him prosper in everything he does. Look how rich he is! But reach out and take away everything he has, and he will surely curse you to your face!" (Job 1:8-11 - NLT).

The tests we go through as believers are evidence of God's involvement in our lives. These should be moments when we get closer rather than distance ourselves from the Creator. God will permit suffering to reveal His glory. In fact, bad things can happen to good people, but God is still in charge. Oftentimes, it becomes clear that man's wisdom is insufficient to make the right judgment when considering the supremacy of God. Satan will attack but God preserves.

It was Job's devotion to God that sustained him amid the attacks. He showed solid character in adversity which was evidence of his relationship with God. He became the focus of a wager between God and Satan and, by his faithfulness, put God on display. Suffering is never an excuse to become disloyal to God. God does not need our understanding to select our path, and neither does He owe any explanation for

His actions. Despite the attacks, as a believer, Job continued being a worshipper and showered God with reverence.

As believers, we must continuously trust God's wisdom and character no matter the circumstances. Those who trust and serve God are never exempt from trials. Not knowing the outcome is no cause to relinquish our faith and confidence in God.

BE THANKFUL DESPITE WHAT HAPPENS

Always be joyful. Never stop praying. Be thankful in all circumstances, for this is God's will for you who belong to Christ Jesus. (1 Thessalonians 5:16-18 - NLT).

Knowing God's will may not make it easy to follow in obedience. Obeying God is a choice that must be made irrespective of our opinions on the matter. God will never require what is impossible for us to fulfill. Not only does He set the standard, but He provides the strength to attain the same. Our attitude is always a reflection of the grace we have received and testimony of the fruit of the Spirit that we manifest.

The demands of godliness are not determined or dependent on seasons but His will. The challenges faced should never cause godly character to wane. God expects us to possess an attitude of gratitude that is not dependent on what is happening externally but based on the communion we have fostered with Him internally. Our thankfulness extends more because of our relationship with Him than any promised rewards.

Whereas we demonstrate thankfulness in the good times, it should never be limited to that. We cannot afford to distance ourselves when the situations become unfavorable and unbearable. God is not only ever present, but He is also reliable and supportive.

Each time he said, "My grace is all you need. My power works best in weakness." So now I am glad to boast about my weaknesses, so that the power of Christ can work through me. That's why I take pleasure in my weaknesses, and in the insults, hardships, persecutions, and troubles that I suffer for Christ. For when I am weak, then I am strong. (2 Corinthians 12:9-10 - NLT).

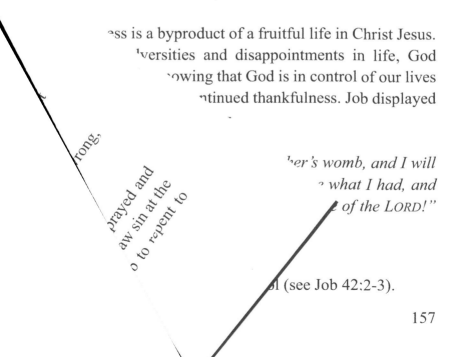

...ess is a byproduct of a fruitful life in Christ Jesus. ...versities and disappointments in life, God ...owing that God is in control of our lives ...ntinued thankfulness. Job displayed

...her's womb, and I will ... what I had, and ... of the LORD!"

...l (see Job 42:2-3).

2. Satan is subject to God (see Job 1:8).

3. The Lord will vindicate the righteous (see Job 13:18).

4. The value of patient endurance (see Job 19:25-27).

We give great honor to those who endure under suffering. For instance, you know about Job, a man of great endurance. You can see how the Lord was kind to him at the end, for the Lord is full of tenderness and mercy. (James 5:11 - NLT).

Despite Job's obvious grief, he was not angry with God at the tragedy but saw this as an opportunity to be consistent in worship. With animals stolen, farm hands and children killed, he demonstrated that his praise for God was independent of his circumstances. Loss of possession and health did not deter or make him unfaithful.

Job's integrity was questioned by others during this time of crisis. He was derided by his friends who came to visit bu still held firm.

1. The first alluded that he had done something w hence his suffering.

2. The other contended that he could have been delivered if he was righteous. He s root of the suffering and required Jo' experience a turnaround.

3. The third denied Job's claim of innocence and dared to say that Job deserved even more punishment from God.

Job's friends viewed his condition with head and not heart and so gave wrong advice 80% of the time. God's plans are often beyond our understanding, and it is futile to challenge His wisdom or actions. Job exhibited much patience and great humility.

Then the LORD said to Job, "Do you still want to argue with the Almighty? You are God's critic, but do you have the answers?" (Job 40:1-2 - NLT).

What we learn from the Book of Job:

- Everyone stands guilty before God in words, thoughts, and deeds.
- Don't compare your life with others.
- Don't dwell on the why question, especially when going through life's challenges.
- Remember compassion when dealing with others.
- Walk always with humility.

CHAPTER 15

PERSPECTIVES: REFLECTIONS AND RESPONSES

My local church was one of three that united to bring Bishop Valentine Rodney to Toronto, Canada to speak. One week into his coming to Toronto, the man of God became ill. It was very upsetting because the man of God was away from home and family.

At first, I did not believe the seriousness of the illness, but when my wife and I went to the Brampton Civic Hospital to relieve Pastor Sophia Martin (who had been there all night), I saw firsthand the seriousness of the illness. Although Bishop was talking, I could see a difference in his personality and a deep concern set into my heart.

I watched them wheel him into the x-ray room, and immediately, the Holy Spirit assured me that he would be okay, and that alleviated my concern and pushed me into prayer mode. Throughout the period that Bishop Rodney was in the hospital, the church never ceased to pray for him, but there was always the underlining feeling of comfort in knowing that God had him and that this sickness was not going to alter him in any way. The prayers were more of thanksgiving that petition.

I must commend Pastor Sophia Martin for her diligent care of Bishop Rodney. She is a real soldier who is loving and caring, and God could not have placed Bishop in better hands during this time of crisis. May God truly bless her.

I am writing this report to document my experiences with a beloved pastor, Rodney, who recently fell ill and was admitted to the hospital. This unforeseen event has triggered a rollercoaster of emotions within me, ranging from brokenness and sadness to disbelief and hopefulness.

The news of Pastor Rodney falling sick came as a sudden blow, shattering my sense of normalcy and security. The initial moments were filled with shock and disbelief as I struggled to come to terms with the stark reality of the situation. The feeling of helplessness and vulnerability was overwhelming, leaving me grappling with a deep sense of sadness and worry.

Navigating through the waves of emotion proved to be a challenging journey. The sight of Pastor Rodney in a hospital bed, surrounded by medical equipment and receiving treatment, tugged at my heartstrings and reinforced the fragility of life. I found myself oscillating between moments of despair and flickers of hope, clinging to the belief that strength and resilience would prevail in Christ.

Despite the dark cloud that loomed overhead, there were glimpses of hope that pierced through the gloom of my emotions. Witnessing the dedication and expertise of the healthcare professionals tending to him instilled a sense of optimism within me. His unwavering commitment and compassion about the sermon he preached on Sunday morning—the evidence of God when we put our trust in Him and believe in Him—gave me hope. I have this hope in Christ despite uncertainty; seeing him lying in the hospital with all the equipment hooked up to him fueled my belief in the power of God. I am a person of faith, and I never stop praying or wavering in my faith in God for him because I believe in the healing power of God. That is why the last sermon he preached resonated with me so much. I know I can trust God for him to receive his healing because my sister just got healed from cancer a few months ago last year.

So, I believe in the evidence that he so passionately preaches. I know, too, that I have the evidence, and I was uplifted by Christ, who healed my sister. I trust in God to do the same for him because I believe in faith with God.

Now faith is the substance of things hoped for, the evidence of things not seen. (Hebrews 11:1 – KJV).

My experience with Pastor Rodney falling ill and being hospitalized has been a poignant journey marked by a whirlwind of emotions. While the road ahead may be fraught with challenges and obstacles, I am holding on to the thread of hope that weaves through this narrative. As I continue to pray for him and offer my consolation and support, I remain steadfast in my belief that brighter days are on the horizon for him. He has lived by the words he preaches, and I believe in the evidence of his faith in God.

Pastor Noel and Dorett Richards
Restoration Christian Ministries

I spoke to my father on the Tuesday before the stroke, and he fell into a deep sleep, which never usually happens, so I allowed him to rest. I called back on Wednesday, but I didn't get a response. I called back twice on Thursday, but there was no response, and I called three times on Friday.

I first wondered if he just needed to focus on the word, but by Friday, I was confused as to why there was no response.

On Saturday, after returning from a fruitful evangelism session, I quickly rushed home to complete an interview, and I got a call. My mum said, "Pray for your dad because he is very sick."

Silence and concern washed over my body. I ran to clear my mind and, in tears and a bit of panic, asked God, "How should I pray about this?" I was quite angry, but God reminded me of Psalm 124: *"I will lift up mine eyes unto the hills, from whence cometh my help. My help cometh from the Lord, which made heaven and earth. He will not suffer thy foot to be moved: he that keepeth thee will not slumber. Behold, he that keepeth Israel shall neither slumber nor sleep. The Lord is thy keeper: the Lord is thy shade upon thy right hand. The sun shall not smite thee by day, nor the moon by night. The Lord shall preserve thee from all evil: he shall preserve thy soul. The Lord shall preserve thy going out and thy coming in from this time forth, and even for evermore." (KJV).*

Immediately, I thanked God for the word and stood firm in it. I reminded Him that my father was serving Him wholeheartedly. God is not a man that He should lie, so I asked God to continue the perfect work that He had started, and, in that moment, my faith was renewed.

Months and weeks before I heard the news from my mother, I played the song repetitively, "What God Can't Do Doesn't Exist." That song spoke about people who would have suffered greatly but God had come through. I also listened to the song "You I Live For" by Moses Bliss. These two songs held me up in this season because they emphasised the power of God being higher than any earthly decree. God had the final say, and we live under His Kingdom.

After receiving the news that my dad had a stroke, I was finally permitted to speak to him. Seeing my jovial, hilarious dad—who is usually dancing, singing, and cracking jokes—in tubes and tired after a few minutes of speaking brought tears to my eyes. My faith remained unshaken, but my heart was broken. I asked God, "Why must You carry my dad through this now? Is this to teach a lesson? If it is, it's a crude one. Things are already rocky, and this, God? This took more than the cake, but God, I trust that You will recover Him because You have not finished Your work in him."

I surrendered my emotions and will to God at that moment because He promised He would be with me and would never forsake me.

This may sound like church talk, but once you see God heal and provide amid chaos, He becomes your comfort. Your faith naturally will begin to rise.

I received calls from family members and friends checking in on me. Although it was well-meaning, I had already left it in God's hands, and it felt like reopening a case that God had already solved. I reassured them that what God can't do, does not exist, and I went back to believing.

Another part of my faith came in because the same God who was able to heal my flu in two days, provide 100% for my education, and a job out of thin air could heal my dad. I had zero doubts that God would finish what He started, and thus, when I witnessed my father leave the hospital room, I went into a period of rejoicing and gratitude. I reposted the video on my Facebook page and stated the song again: " What God Can't Do Does Not Exist!"

God never goes back on His Word. What He started, He will perform to completion. When waiting on God, I encourage you to ask His will over a situation, rejoice, and stand firm in the salvation of the Lord. He will finish what He has started.

Zharia R-I Rodney MSc (Aston), BSc. (U.W.I.)
Content Creator, Mindset Coach

This is my documentation of our account of what took place and our response to the news that Bishop Valentine Rodney suddenly fell ill. On Sunday, 7th of April 2024, I received a message via WhatsApp from Pastor Jennifer Samuels, who resides in the United States of America, asking for urgent prayers to be made in relation to Bishop Valentine Rodney. The report was that Bishop Rodney had a stroke while preaching at a church and was rushed to the hospital. I immediately informed my wife, Pastor Melody Palmer, because for the past two years, we have been calling the name of pastors before the Lord every morning in our time of prayer.

Because the information wasn't very clear, I set out to get some confirmation and ascertain its accuracy. We must wage war with knowledge and not based on ignorance (see Luke 14:31-32). I made a call to Pastor Winston Brown, a close friend of both Bishop and myself, and through him, I learnt that Bishop was not in Jamaica but in Canada. He told me that he gathered that Bishop Valentine Rodney had a stroke or something to that effect, and his wife was on her way to him as we spoke.

My thirty-nine years of experience with the Lord has taught me that we needed to throw down the chief prince (see Ephesians 6:12) over that region using Paul's recommendation, i.e., "Praying with all kinds of prayer" (see Ephesians 6:18). We have at least fifteen kinds of prayer at our disposal. I immediately started to mobilize teams of local and international prayer groups to multiply the warfare against the enemy (see Deuteronomy 32:30, Joshua 23:10). We needed a little more than just faith; we needed an element of quantum physics and exponential math in defense of my brother and friend, Bishop Valentine Rodney.

Although the information was still sketchy then, we would leave nothing to chance. I sent out messages to several pastors, including the Spanish Town Ministers Fraternal, to get them on board. I needed to have tactics where "Altars speak to Altars," "Mountain speak to Mountain," and "Authority speak to Authority" (see Deuteronomy 27:11-13, 1 Kings 18:23-24, 31-39). I had no contact information for Bishop's wife, so I could not contact her directly, but we kept praying; the church kept praying (see Acts 12:5) throughout the rest of that day, Sunday the 7th of April and continuing into Monday all day.

As a church (Jubilee Worship Centre, of which I am senior pastor), our Bible study is held online via Zoom on Monday nights and transcends denominational boundaries, with attendees numbering up to seventy, spanning Jamaica, the British Virgin Islands (BVI), the Cayman Islands, the United States of America (USA), and the United Kingdom, and as far as Japan.

We made this news a point of duty, a call to arms, a clarion call for that first hour of the prayer meeting and Bible study, to have Bishop's name raised and announced before the throne of the Lord, praying without ceasing. The aim again was multiplying the warfare against the enemy on behalf of our friend.

At 10:30 PM, the end of our Bible study that night, Monday 8th April 2024, we again prayed for Bishop Valentine Rodney. Each person was admonished to continue praying and to get others to pray until the miracle was complete. We were still working with the information we had that it was a stroke.

On the 10th of April 2024, the first picture emerged of Bishop Valentine Rodney in a hospital bed in Canada. My assessment of the picture and the position in which he lay led me to believe, at the time, that even if he had a stroke, he had not gone into a state of paralysis where any of his limbs were contorted, and his face was twisted.

I again updated the teams on this assessment, and we continued to pray using that picture as a point of contact. At some point, we learned that he was dealing with a blood clot or brain aneurysm, which caused the stroke. I again updated the teams, targeting our prayer around those areas and presenting a case (intercession) before God concerning the man of God and his assignment, mission, purpose, and mandate to the nations and the kingdom of God.

On the 13th of April, a video was sent to me from Facebook of Bishop Rodney in his bed, glasses on, being coherent, presenting a case concerning the resurrection of Jesus with the tagline: "Show me the evidence." In that video, he made it clear that the song that says "An empty grave is there to prove my saviour lives" was not the actual evidence but rather "A living, breathing, moving body; the bodily resurrection of Jesus was that evidence." I took that as the battering ram for the next stage of the warfare. In the back of my mind, I was working with 1 Timothy 1:18-20, which instructs us not to fight for our prophecy but to use our prophecy as a weapon in our war to fulfill our purpose. I again crafted another message, sent it out with the video to the teams, and instructed them on our WhatsApp channels again, with over seventy persons spanning Jamaica to Japan.

At this point, I pulled in friends in Africa to pray, "Lord, show us the evidence." (see 2 Corinthians 12:4-6). We wanted evidence of the resurrection of Jesus at work in our brother and Bishop's life. The scripture says in Romans 8:11, *"The Spirit of God, who raised Jesus from the dead, lives in you. And just as God raised Christ Jesus from the dead, he will give life to your mortal bodies by this same Spirit living within you." (NLT).* So our prayer was, "Lord, show us the evidence of Your resurrection power. Show us the evidence of a quickened body, that Your servant will be restored speedily to full health without any form of paralysis, any form of weakness, any brain damage, any form of slurred speech, any form of diminishment in his vision/his eyesight or any such thing."

We doubled down on our prayer meeting and Bible study on April 22nd, 2024, and continued praying along those lines. At some point between the 12th and 23rd of April 2024, I learnt that the church where Bishop was speaking where the incident happened was that of one of my spiritual daughters, Prophetess Sophia Martin, so I reached out to her to find out how Bishop Rodney was doing. I was told that on that very day of my calling her, he was to leave the specialized hospital that deals with brain-related matters and should return on the 24th of April 2024 back to the first hospital where he was taken when the incident happened.

I was told he was coherent, moving around, talking, and walking, and that his return to this hospital was a matter of procedure to ensure that, through physiotherapy, he would regain full body mobility.

Again, I updated the teams and crafted another message to send out again: "The evidence of the resurrection power has now manifested. We should now move into thanksgiving mode because God has heard and answered our prayers."

Even though we received this good news and saw evidence of him the following day in a wheelchair, we were relentless. It is important for us to know that Jesus taught us one of the methods of prayer. He said we should:

- ask and keep on asking.
- knock and keep on knocking.
- seek and keep on seeking because.
- 100% of those who ask will receive 100% of the time.
- 100% of those who knock, the door will 100% open to them at that time.
- 100% of those who seek, 100% of the time receive what they sought from the Lord's hand.[2]

Everyone must know that our brother and friend, Bishop Valentine Rodney, is a living, breathing, walking, miraculous testimony of what the power of God can do when the church prays.

I close with something that the Apostle Paul said. He says, "I want to know Christ—that I may know Him. I want to know the Holy Spirit. I want to know Christ's suffering and to conform to Christ's death. I want to know the Holy Spirit

---

[2] Matthew 7:7-8

in an intimate fellowship. He is the power. He is the one who raised Christ from the dead." (see Philippians 3:10-12).

Apostle Wayne EA Palmer
Senior Pastor
Jubilee Worship Centre
Marriage Officer, JP and Lay Magistrate

On March 29th, 2024, I went to Jamaica for two weddings: one on the 30th and the second on April 7th. On Monday, April 01, 2024, I visited my brother, Bishop Valentine Rodney's home in his absence. His wife and younger daughter were present. Mrs. Rodney called her husband. My brother and I spoke on the phone. While talking to him on the phone, the Lord led me to pray for him and his family.

I was very obedient to the voice of the Lord and His assignment for me. I walked around the parameter of the property, praying, declaring and pleading the blood of Jesus, while my brother was still on the other end of the phone. For the next two days, I was in communication with him.

On Friday night, I just got into my sister-in-law's house when I was receiving a call from Canada. I did not answer as I was not roaming. While trying to call back on WhatsApp, the phone rang again. The caller was Apostle Sophia Martin, a friend of mine. Sophia stated, "You know your brother is here in Canada preaching right?"

I responded, "Yes, I know."

"He has not been feeling well," she said.

She said on Wednesday, he complained of a headache. They took him to the doctor, and he was diagnosed with a throat infection. She continued to say he took the medication, but he was vomiting. He went to use the restroom, and they heard a big commotion. They went to check on him. He was unable to walk unassisted and was somewhat confused. She said she got a call from the house where he was staying, stating he was getting worse. She told me she was on her way from preaching at the church where he was to preach. She went to get him and took him to the hospital. I said to her, "Sophia, are you guys sure he did not get a stroke?" I told her to keep me up to date. As soon as I hung up, I started to pray for my brother. When I was finished, my sister-in-law asked what was wrong. I told her, and she started to pray for my brother immediately.

I kept in touch with Sophia throughout the night. I went to bed at 3am and got up at 5am to follow up with Sophia again. At about 8am, Sophia video-called me and showed me my brother. She stated that he was doing much better. She allowed him to see me, and I told him it was going to be okay. He said that was what Sophia said. I asked about his blood pressure, and when I heard the numbers, I was concerned because it was too high. I was told that it has been high since he got there. I was trying to find out what they were doing about it. As a registered nurse, I knew the numbers were not good.

I called my brother's wife afterward to let her know what was happening because she was not aware. I ensured that I video-called her and broke the news in a subtle way. She was indeed astonished. The hospital in Brampton reached out to the hospital in Mississauga, and they told them to do a CT scan of the brain to rule out stroke. It was a weekend, so they took a while to read the results. Apostle Sophia did not want to leave Bishop at the hospital by himself, but I begged her to go home and take some rest. She had been at the hospital from Friday night with him.

The following morning, I called Apostle. She was on her way to the hospital and promised to call me when she got there. It was April 7th—my son, Jabari's birthday—and the day of my batchmate from nursing school's wedding. I got a video-call from Sophia, and she was bawling. She stated, "June, it bad. It bad. They moved him to the other hospital in Mississauga. He is on a breathing machine. You must come."

I said to her, "Okay, Sophia. It's going to be okay." I had a calm in my spirit. I told her to call me when she got to the next hospital.

I video-called Mrs. Rodney, telling her all that I was told. I said to her, "Yevett, you have to go to Canada ASAP." She started to cry. I could not stay on the phone with her because

I did not want her to break me. I told her to call her bestie and pour out on her. I then called my siblings and updated them on what was happening. Sophia called to let me know that they bore a hole in his head to drain the fluids and that he had a massive stroke. I saw a picture of him and realized he was incubated and was placed in a medical coma. I was not sure what kind of stroke it was, whether it was hemorrhagic or ischemic. I called my ARNP friend, and we spoke. She said, "June, you have to go. I will buy your ticket." I was a bit overwhelmed, so I asked her to check the flights and purchase the earliest one.

At this time, I was trying to get on the evening flight to go home and then leave from the USA to Canada because all I had with me was summer clothes. There were no available seats for that evening, so I went to the wedding. I must say, Apostle R. J. Edwards and the Light House Assembly petitioned heaven on Valentine Rodney's behalf. My next job was to tactfully share information about her firstborn with our mother. I had to bear in mind that our mother was hypertensive, and we did not want to shock her into a stroke as well.

In the middle of everything, God was truly at work orchestrating everything for our good. Yevett and I got our tickets, and my husband took us to the airport in Montego Bay; thank God. Sophia called, smiling and saying he was doing great and that he was not on the breathing machine anymore. We got to Canada on Monday the 8th, sometime after 7 pm, and went straight to the hospital. When we got to the hospital, I spoke with the nurse, who gave us an update. She stated that when she did the neuro check, he did not remember some things. I asked for an example. She said he didn't remember the day and month. I said, "Ma'am, half the time, I don't know what day it is either, plus it's a new month, so I am not worried about that." I asked why we needed to wear a gown and they said he had the flu.

When we went into the room, he did not turn his head to look. I rubbed his face while standing on his left side. He furrowed his brow. I asked him, "Val, do you know who is speaking to you?"

He said, "Yes."

"Who?"

"Marie."

That is my pet name. I motioned to his wife to go to his right side. I asked, "Do you know who that is?"

He squinted and said, "Yvette." He told me he married the prettiest girl in the world. I noticed on the patient board that it said, "Patient extubated himself."

The next morning, we went to the hospital to visit him. I spoke with the intensivist to get an update on my brother. The doctor mentioned that he had extubated himself but was doing great. I told him that he was previously diagnosed with sleep apnea and used a CPAP. He said, "Well, there is no evidence of that now." God cured the sleep apnea. I then spoke with the NP for the neurosurgeon. She showed me the CT scan and how swollen the brain was. She said they would continue to drain the brain slowly. That was when I learnt he had an ischemic stroke at the back of the brain,

We went to the hospital every day and spent the day with him. I was very alert to my brother's treatment, ensuring they gave him stool softener and blood thinners. He was making great progress, and I felt that it was safe for me to leave him in the capable hands of his wife. I thank everybody for all the prayers, calls, and all you do for my brother and his family.

June Peters-Brown B.N., M.
Registered Nurse
Mary Kay Sales Director
Evangelist

On Saturday morning, April 6th 2024, my phone began to ring. It was my sister-in-law calling via WhatsApp. She insisted that we should connect via video, so I thought she, being the consummate entrepreneur, wanted to introduce me to another of the products she markets.

June, a registered nurse, began to systematically and clinically give me an account of what was happening to my husband, who was, by that time, admitted to Brampton

Hospital. I was sitting on the recliner chair in my living room. As she unfolded the series of events and developments (my husband losing control of his bodily functions, unable to answer basic questions, unable to walk), I felt my strength literally draining from my body—from my chest down to my lower extremities. My appetite for food also deserted me and did not return for days. I was in utter disbelief. I remember asking her, "Who? Huh? What? Not my husband of twenty-seven years. Not my husband who, even though he had been ill before, had never been so helpless and unable to function without physical assistance. Jesus! Jesus! Jesus!" was all I could muster.

The initial prognosis from the hospital made it worse. It was similarity chillingly reminding me of the diagnosis that took my brother's life a little over three months prior. My mind was in chaos. What was happening? My sister-in-law added at the end that she felt peace in all of this and Valentine would be alright. I could only, in faith, take her word for it. The news had shaken all I prayed, preached, and praised about over the years—standing firmly and unreservedly on the goodness of the miracle-working, healing Jesus.

We connected via phone while Valentine was in hospital that afternoon. He recognised who I was. I spoke with a lilt that I did not feel. "How could you change your accommodations without letting me know?" I jokingly asked.

He answered with his usual matching wit, "Why not?" We spoke at length, and he encouraged me to attend the convention that Saturday, even though all desire to go had deserted me. While we spoke, he also answered a series of questions from the medical team, even adding with his quick-wittedness that he was not pregnant either. At this point, I said to myself that he would be okay.

Sunday morning took a southern turn. June called back, this time a far cry from her matter-of-fact clinical report. She was frantic, and her voice shook with emotion. She blurted out that it was very, very bad. He had to be transferred to another hospital. It did not look good at all! I needed to travel to Canada. Immediately.

I broke down the worst way only after I began to relay the devastating news on the telephone calls I made to a couple of close friends. My world was crashing down. In all of this, I had to keep calm and act normal whenever I was with our youngest.

Everything I did from there to the next two months dramatically changed my life and way of living. You see, every time I traveled, Valentine was the one who always located the flight, booked the ticket, and got me to the airport. Just by booking that flight to Canada myself was a painful realisation that something was very wrong. I was thinking, "Babe would be the one doing this for me." From what was shaping out to be another long two or more weeks of waiting out the time before my husband returned home was now suddenly transported into frantic plans to race to Canada to see my husband alive. I had the task of telling my daughters that their dad was seriously ill. Each had to be told with different levels of details dispensed to assimilate the information without overload. To our eldest, Zharia, I said that her dad was very sick in the hospital and she should pray. Our prayer-warrior daughter replied promptly that she was on it. Her unflinching and unwavering faith in God amazes me even in this difficult time. Our youngest, Ana-Olivia, moved from disbelief to shock, to panic, asking me if her dad was going to die. Though my mind was in turmoil, I reassured her that we were all praying and all would be well.

The situation became graver when a medical team member advised me in Jamaica that I would be contacted if any major decisions were to be made. *What major decisions?* I could, at that point, think of the only decision that needed to be made regarding a patient who was unable to breathe on his own and barely responding at that point. I went to bed with my phone next to me but also dreaded that the phone would ring. I wanted to sleep but didn't want to fall asleep. At least when I was fully awake, I could avert certain thoughts. If I was falling asleep, it would be more difficult to control unwanted and unfavourable scenarios that were threatening to crowd my thinking. I could only cry, "Lord, have mercy!" My prayers, even though sometimes difficult, would almost always end with a submission to the will of God. In this instance, however, all I could cry was, "Lord, have mercy! Lord, help! Lord, deliver!" During the day, I had to interact with several people as I prepared to leave for Canada the next day. I was very calm and compartmentalised in making several arrangements, even driving out of the parish to leave our youngest in the care of family while I was away. That could only be God. He steadied my head and heart even amid this crisis.

The prayers, calls, and messages received from family—my work family, church family, and church leadership—kept me afloat. In the hours and days ahead, I leaned heavily on them. I literally had no choice but to rely on the faithfulness of our Lord, Most High. I could only agree with the declarations of healing and strength that poured in via phone. Exercising my faith was not even my effort, but it was done with the help of God.

I saw the hand and providence of God at work throughout the ordeal, from my sister-in-law being at the right place at the right time to travel with me and offer support and expert advice, to family, church, and work-family providing invaluable support and encouragement in every way.

Pastor Dr. Sophia Martin and her team were the consummate host and an indomitable tower of strength and support despite the stress of it all. Her insistence to personally make the daily trips (sometimes up to three per day) to Mississauga from Brampton, transporting me to and from the hospital for many days, was nothing short of heroic. For the full duration of our stay in Canada, she cared and gave with an open heart that reflects and exudes her fierce love for God and His people.

As we were led past several rooms in the Intensive Care Unit to get to the one where my husband lay, I decided I was not going to be distracted or disheartened by what I might see in those rooms, so I looked neither right nor left. Seeing Valentine immobile and all strung up to a plethora of machines by a network of wires was daunting. But just getting there, finally, and being able to talk to him and hold his hand was a huge relief. He spoke little that first night upon our arrival but still managed to weave wit in his responses to his sister and me. That was the husband I knew and love.

God was unfolding to me, day by day, that His plans concerning my husband did not end at that hospital, even though for the first few nights, I broke down when I was by myself in the bedroom that hosted my husband each time I looked at his personal effects, clothing, etc. and wondering if he would ever need or use them the same way he had before he became ill. I was fine while I was by his bed watching him (and the readings from the machines), feeding him and administering moisturisers each day. I had anxious moments when I left his bed at night, especially when I was alone. The Lord had to remind me that He was in control, not I. Trust in God was all I could do. It was the only thing I knew how to do. This entire experience taught me effectual, fervent praying on another level. It depended not on how loud my voice became or how long my prayers lasted but my real and raw honesty, complete trust, and reliance upon the Omnipotent God's will, wonder, goodness, and mercy.

My husband's road to recovery was/is nothing short of miraculous. His first steps were amazing, partly because of the concentration he had to engage in. He had lost the ability to walk and had to remind himself how to do it, "Put one foot forward, then the other." Day two of moving saw Valentine walking around half the block of the ICU, aided by a walker.

During this time, my husband and I were further amazed by the outpouring of love and care in every way from near and far. We received hundreds of calls and messages from all over. It was many times an impossible task to manage and respond to them all; we remain humbled and beyond grateful.

Everything that transpired and everyone I encountered made me realize even more starkly how great God is. God masterfully orchestrated and coordinated lives and events far more interestingly and perfectly than any planner could. God, the Master Strategist, had extraordinarily woven this wondrous tapestry of every person involved and affected to converge in April/May 2024. Strangers and acquaintances became friends, who quickly became family. Old friends and families were reunited. My cousin, whom I had not seen or spoken to for over twenty years, connected with us and kindly transported me from the hospital for a portion of the time. When work prevented him, he had a network of persons ready to fill the gap. Favour was plenty.

The hospital where my husband stayed was home to the best neuro-consultants in that region of Canada. That was by God's design. The medical personnel's care and attention to detail were second to none. That is by God's design.

Ministry moments expanded, invaluable connections were forged, and meaningful friendships were formed. I could not, still cannot and will not, be able to grasp fully how awesome God is in all His ways, even the ones that cause us much pain and panic. God, to me, is just out-of-this-world in His doings, yet so near to His people. His love, purposes, will, and ways are perfect. They are past finding out. I can only say, "Thank You, Lord, for showing evidence of Your sovereignty yet again. I stand in awe of You!"

Yevett Thomas-Rodney CA, FCA, MBA
Minister of Religion

CHAPTER 16

THE FIRES AFTERMATH

It is obvious that not by a long shot is the story concluded. God is still writing my story, and there are still chapters with multiple experiences to be added. God's sovereignty is on display as He purposefully guides and navigates me towards the future. The outcome is already guaranteed; He will receive the glory, and His name will be exalted and displayed. Everything that happened was most definitely a part of the divine plan. Boundaries and parameters were set, and a determination was made concerning what would happen and the outcome.

There were those who were overly concerned that my planned departure from Canada was too early and that I should have spent additional months in the name of recovery. I simply stated to them that the doctors had written in the notes received after discharge that I would be fit to travel after four weeks. My darling wife made the arrangements for us to travel via Air Canada on the 27th of May, 2024. I was regaining strength fast and was far more confident in my gait. However, as a precautionary measure, wheelchair assistance was booked to facilitate ease of movement through the airports.

We believe a miracle had occurred, but time was needed for a much fuller recovery. A miraculous encounter with Jesus will thrust you back into the everyday activities of life.

Holding her hand, he said to her, "Talitha koum," which means "Little girl, get up!" And the girl, who was twelve years old, immediately stood up and walked around! They were overwhelmed and totally amazed. Jesus gave them strict orders not to tell anyone what had happened, and then he told them to give her something to eat. (Mark 5:41-43 - NLT).

His first statement was to address the situation from a spiritual perspective so that life could be restored. However, the second statement deals with the physical needs of nutrition that had to be met. Life returned must be maintained. The provision of physical food would cause her to become stronger and was a necessary form of sustenance.

Let us consider that regaining strength and rhythm of movements will take time and of course adequate nutrition, exercise, and rest will be needed. There are basic rules and regimens that must be followed in order to avoid a relapse that could, in the eyes of many, cause a shred of doubt to be cast on the authenticity of the miracle that had taken place.

The surgeons operated, but God provided healing and wellness over time.

The man who was healed at Bethesda was warned by Jesus that unless he dealt with the root cause of his illness, something more fatal might occur. It is important that we avoid falling into the trap of not observing proper health protocols because the major crisis is past. Sometimes a change of habits is required to walk in the healing that has been received. It makes no sense to throw caution to the wind. In many instances, there is a need to listen to and follow the advice of health care providers. Receiving a miracle of healing is one thing (divine), but maintaining a healthy lifestyle is another (physical and natural).

The man didn't know, for Jesus had disappeared into the crowd. But afterward Jesus found him in the Temple and told him, "Now you are well; so stop sinning, or something even worse may happen to you." Then the man went and told the Jewish leaders that it was Jesus who had healed him. (John 5:13-15 - NLT).

After discharge from the hospital, I had headaches daily and had to resort to prescription medication for relief. The doctors had prescribed a daily regimen of aspirin and blood pressure medication, with pain medication taken on an as-needed basis. The day of the return flight to Jamaica, I had no such headaches, and neither did the pressurised cabin and the flight at high altitudes have any negative effect. My wife would constantly ask me if all was well, to which I would reply that I was okay.

I had to settle down to a far less hectic schedule than what I had become accustomed to over the years. My major focus was rebuilding the immune system through a regulated diet, getting sufficient rest, exercise, taking the medication prescribed by the doctors and certainly not rushing back into ministry activities at a high level.

I visited my personal physician, who did some checks and gave some recommendations to be followed to assist in the overall recovery. This included exercise at least five days a week for a minimum of thirty minutes a day. I recalled that one of the strong recommendations from the doctors at THP Hospital in Mississauga was that walking is an important form of exercise. The walking certainly helped, and I looked so much younger to many. The sickness had ravaged the body, but God proved Himself to be a restorer. The trauma felt by the body can cause one to age or affect movements. God was not just concerned with my health care within the hospital but my aftercare subsequent to discharge. God wants you not just to be healed but to be made whole.

But Jesus turned him about, and when he saw her, he said, Daughter, be of good comfort; thy faith hath made thee whole. And the woman was made whole from that hour. (Matthew 9:22 - KJV).

When Jesus saw him lie, and knew that he had been now a long time in that case, he saith unto him, Wilt thou be made whole? (John 5:6 - KJV).

The doctor also recommended that I do an MRI as a follow-up so that an adequate assessment can be made regarding my progress. The doctor was pleased with the results, which implied that the healing was in earnest.

One of the major challenges that had to be overcome was driving and reapproaching the pulpit ministry. There was always the thought voiced by others that more time was needed to venture forth. My conviction was, it had to be tackled to avoid fear stepping in. There was some anxiety about accepting and fulfilling the first engagement, which required a two-hour drive, then ministry. Not surprisingly, it went well, and I believe that if God could cause me to recover from a near-death experience, then this was easy for Him. My confidence has risen with each engagement as I keep trusting God in the accomplishment of His will for my life.

The fulfillment of my assignment continues not just to Jamaica but beyond as God directs my path.

And I am certain that God, who began the good work within you, will continue his work until it is finally finished on the day when Christ Jesus returns. (Philippians 1:6 - NLT).

CHAPTER 17

ANATOMY OF A STROKE

UNDERSTANDING AND DEALING WITH A STROKE

The Word of God in Hosea 4:6 says, "My people are destroyed for lack of knowledge." (KJV). In this chapter, I will attempt to provide the knowledge required to inform, advise, and ultimately prevent this potentially catastrophic condition, as well as improve the lives of those who have suffered a stroke.

So, what is a stroke? The medical term for this condition is cerebrovascular accident. Cerebro refers to the brain, vascular refers to blood vessels, and accident refers to the event. In order words, this is a disease involving the arteries (blood vessels) leading to the brain and those within the brain. These arteries make up the blood supply to the brain and are responsible for carrying oxygen and nutrients to the brain cells.

A stroke occurs when blood flow in one of these vessels is blocked by a blood clot or by the bursting or rupturing of one of these vessels. When either occurs, the part of the brain supplied by the affected vessel no longer receives the oxygen and nutrients it needs, so that part of the brain actually dies. How this affects the individual depends on the part of the brain affected and the size of the damage.

Strokes involving the obstruction of blood flow within an artery by a blood clot are called an ischemic stroke. About 87% of all strokes are ischemic. A stroke caused by blood vessel rupture or burst is referred to as a haemorrhagic stroke.

Stroke is the number one cause of death in Jamaica based on figures collated in 2019, accounting for 13% of deaths. In the United States, 1 in 6 deaths (17.5%) from cardiovascular disease was due to stroke in figures for 2022.

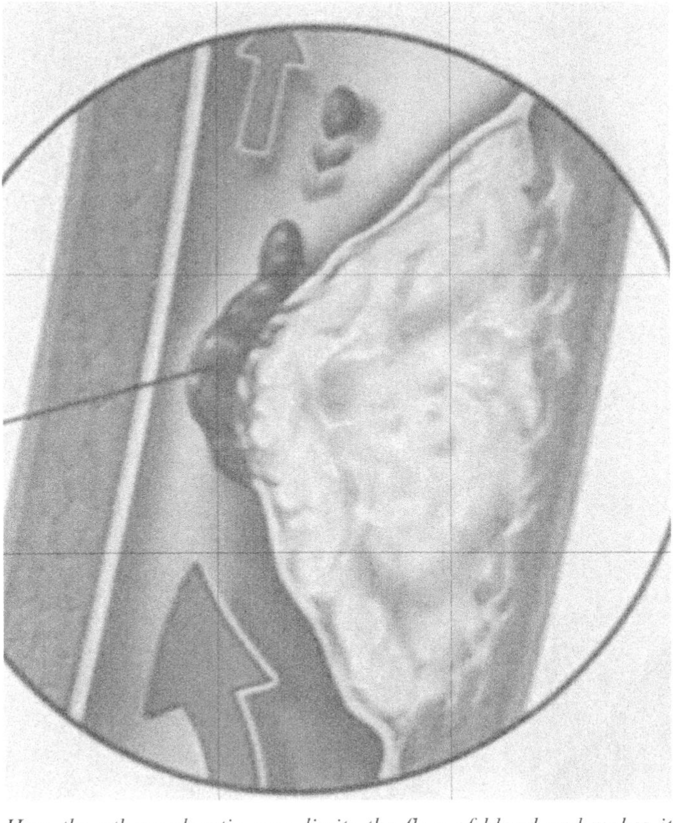

Here the atherosclerotic area limits the flow of blood and makes it easy for blood to block the remaining area in the blood vessel causing a stroke.

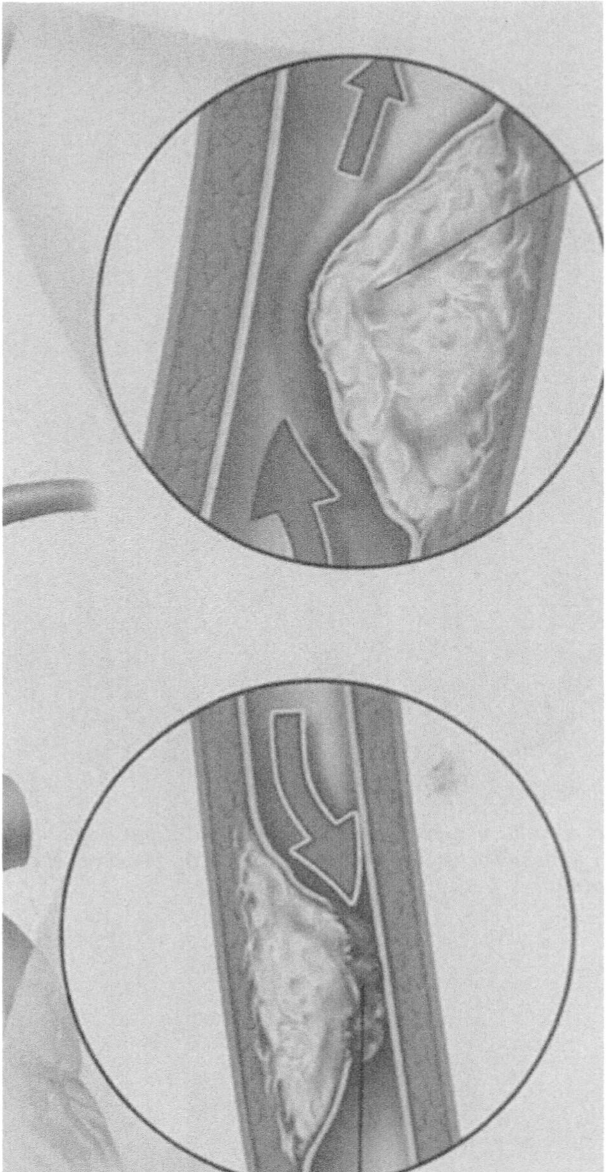

CAUSES

An ischemic stroke is caused by the development of fatty plaques within the arterial wall. This is called atherosclerosis. These deposits are made up of cholesterol, fatty substances, cellular waste products, calcium, and fibrin, a clotting material in the blood. As plaque builds up, the wall of the blood vessel thickens or hardens. This build-up narrows the channel within the artery, reducing blood flow. That lessens the amount of oxygen and other nutrients reaching the body.

Atherosclerosis is a slow, lifelong progression of changes in the blood vessels that may start in childhood and get worse faster as you age.

Many scientists believe plaque begins when an artery's inner lining becomes damaged.

FOUR POSSIBLE CAUSES OF SUCH DAMAGE ARE:

- Elevated levels of fats in the blood.
- Hypertension
- Smoking
- Diabetes

Smoking can speed up the progression of plaques.

The most common cause of a hemorrhagic stroke is hypertension. This is especially true when a person's blood pressure is very high, stays high for a long time, or both. Other conditions or causes of hemorrhagic strokes include:

- Brain aneurysm (abnormal bulging of a blood vessel wall in places where it's weaker than normal).
- Brain tumours.
- Other conditions that involve weakened blood vessels in your brain, such as cerebral amyloid angiopathy.
- Blood-thinning medications (these can cause bleeding in your brain or make it worse).
- Head injuries.

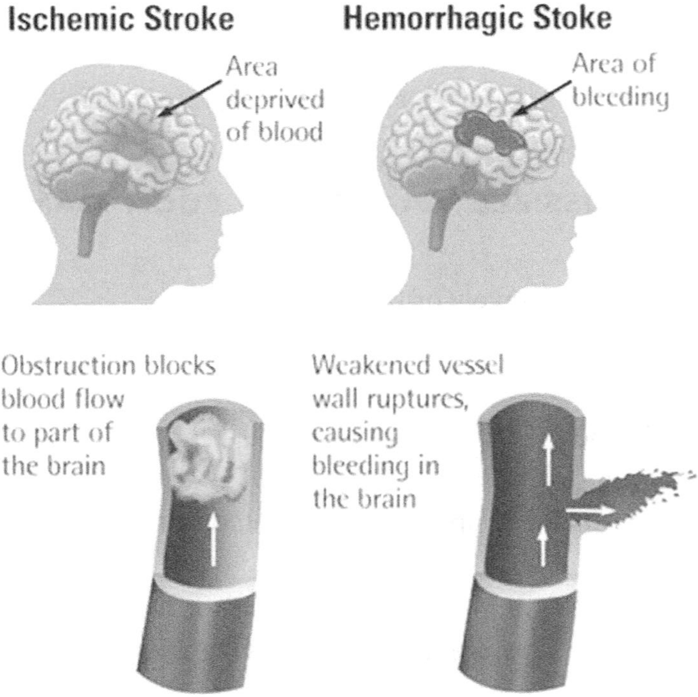

SYMPTOMS OF A STROKE

The effects of a stroke can range from barely perceptible to fatality. In between, there are varying presentations that sometimes improve over time.

Symptoms can vary depending on the area of the brain affected. Symptoms may include sudden onset of:

- Weakness or sensory charges: sudden weakness, numbness, or tingling in the face, arm, or leg (usually on one side of the body).
- Trouble speaking, sudden loss of speech, difficulty finding words, slurred speech, or trouble reading, writing, or understanding speech.
- Vision Problems: sudden loss of vision in one eye, loss of peripheral vision on one side, or double vision.
- Dizziness: sudden spinning, dizziness, loss of balance or coordination, unsteadiness with walking, sudden confusion.
- Headaches that are severe and without known cause.

RISK FACTORS

What is a transient ischemic attack (TIA)? This is a temporary blockade of arteries. This puts the person at greater risk of suffering another stroke. TIA is a brief or mini-stroke that occurs when the blood flow to the brain is temporarily disrupted and then resolves. Symptoms may last for only a few minutes or up to 24 hours. It is an important warning sign that you may be at risk of having a stroke in the future. It is therefore important to reduce your risks to prevent a stroke.

RISK FACTORS THAT CANNOT BE MODIFIED:

- Increased age.
- Family history of stroke.
- Race (Asian or African ancestry).
- Male sex.
- Previous transient ischemic attack or previous stroke.

COMPLICATIONS

Stroke may lead to severe complications:

- Paralysis or loss of muscle movement: Patient may become paralyzed on one side of the body or lose control of certain muscles, such as those on one side of the face or one arm.
- Difficulty in talking or swallowing.
- Memory loss or thinking difficulties; it also affects thinking, making judgments, reasoning, and understanding concepts.
- Emotional problems: stroke survivors may develop depression.
- Changes in behaviour and self-care ability: Stroke survivors may become more withdrawn and less social or more impulsive. They may need help with grooming and daily chores. After care is therefore dependent on the extent of the complications being experienced.

Persons who have residual paralysis interfering with normal functioning generally require physiotherapy for varying periods. A speech therapist may also be necessary to assist with speech deficits. Some persons lose the ability to swallow and require a feeding tube for nutrition. With emotional problems, a psychologist may be required to provide support.

PREVENTION

To prevent a stroke, we must address modifiable risk factors.

RISK FACTORS THAT CAN BE MODIFIED:

- High blood pressure.
- High cholesterol.
- An irregular heartbeat (Atrial Fibrillation).
- Heart valve disease or recent heart attack.
- Sedentary lifestyle.
- Excess alcohol use.
- Smoking
- Diabetes Mellitus (sugar).
- Stress

In addressing diet, exercise, and stress, a number of the modifiable factors will automatically be improved, such as hypertension, diabetes, elevated cholesterol, and sedentary lifestyle. Of course, it goes without saying that smoking and excessive alcohol use must be avoided.

Persons with hypertension and diabetes must be diligent in taking their prescribed medications in a bid to maintain normal levels. Heart disease requires intervention from a heart specialist (Cardiologist), and appropriate treatments (medication) can greatly improve your prognosis.

Let us address some modifiable factors which have far-reaching implications.

HOW TO MANAGE STRESS

What is stress? Stress is your body's response to a challenge or demand. Everyone experiences stress, which can be triggered by a range of events, from small daily hassles to major changes.

HOW CAN WE HANDLE STRESS IN HEALTHY WAYS?

Stress serves an important purpose—it enables us to respond quickly to threats and avoid danger. However, lengthy exposure to stress may lead to mental health difficulties and actual physical ailments requiring treatment. A body of research suggests that increased stress levels interfere with your ability to deal with physical illness.

Although it is impossible to avoid all stress, one can work on handling (managing) stress in healthy ways, thereby increasing your potential to recover.

1. **Eat and drink to optimize your health.**

Some people try to reduce stress by drinking alcohol or eating too much. These actions may seem to help at the moment but may add to stress in the long run. Caffeine also can compound the effects of stress. Consuming a healthy, balanced diet can help to combat the effects of stress.

WHAT IS A HEALTHY DIET?

This is a diet that provides all the nutrients, vitamins, and minerals that a person needs to stay healthy and function. A balanced diet includes foods from different groups, such as protein, carbohydrates, fats, fruits, and vegetables.

These include:

- Staples like cereals (wheat, barley, rye, maize, or rice), starchy tubers, or roots (potato, yam, taro or cassava).
- Legumes (lentils and beans).
- Fruit and vegetables.
- Foods from animal sources (meat, fish, eggs, and milk).

A balanced diet also has the right number of calories for a person's weight. Avoids processed foods.

WHAT ARE PROCESSED FOODS?

Any food that is changed from its natural state by varying processes (canning, freezing, frying, heating, chopping, milling, blanching, cooking, packaging, etc). Processed foods may also have added ingredients such as preservatives, flavours, salt, sugar, or fats.

Some are minimally processed, retaining most of their original properties, while others are heavily processed and may be unhealthy due to high levels of salt and sugar. Some examples are canned tomatoes, frozen fruits, roasted nuts, sliced vegetables, bagged salad, and baked goods.

PROCESSED FOODS TO AVOID

Processed meats such as sausage, bacon, and pepperoni are all high in fats and promote cancer.

Baked products such as cookies, pastries, and cakes are loaded with calories with no nutrients, refined sugars, and white flour, causing obesity and diseases like diabetes.

White bread is made from refined flour which has empty calories and is just as effective as table sugar. All nutrients in whole wheat have been exposed to grinding and processing. Eat Ezekiel bread or whole grain bread instead.

Avoid sugary drinks, french fries or potato chips, fast food meats, vegetable oils (soybean, canola or corn), margarine (which is engineered food high in refined oils), and trans fat (which is toxic). Use real butter.
Applying these recommendations can lower the risk of disease and enhance general health.

2. **Exercise regularly**

In addition to having physical health benefits, exercise is a powerful means of relieving stress. Consider aerobic exercise, strengthening with weights, or movement activities like cycling or playing a sport. Be sure to set reasonable goals for yourself. Aerobic exercise has been shown to release endorphins, which are natural substances that help you feel better and maintain a positive attitude.

Get at least 150 minutes of moderate aerobic activity or 75 minutes of vigorous aerobic activity a week, or a combination of moderate and vigorous activity. The guidelines suggest that you spread out this exercise during a week. To provide even greater health benefits and to assist with weight loss or maintaining weight loss, at least 300 minutes a week is recommended. But even small amounts of physical activity are helpful.

Being active for short periods of time throughout the day can add up to provide health benefits.

Do strength training exercises for all major muscle groups at least twice weekly. Aim to do a single set of each exercise using a weight or resistance level heavy enough to tire your muscles after about 12 to 15 repetitions.

Moderate aerobic exercise includes brisk walking, biking, swimming, and lawn mowing. Vigorous aerobic exercise includes activities such as running, heavy yard work, and aerobic dancing. Strength training can include using weight machines, your body weight, heavy bags, resistance tubing or resistance paddles in the water, or activities such as playing football.

Persons with disabilities can do simple chair exercises like air punching.

BENEFITS OF EXERCISE

- Reduce the development of chronic illnesses like hypertension or diabetes and, ultimately, the development of a stroke.
- Control of weight.
- Improves sleep.
- Boosts energy levels.
- Improves mood and helps to destress.

3. **Stop using tobacco and nicotine products.**

People who use nicotine often refer to it as a stress reliever. However, nicotine actually places more stress on your body by increasing physical arousal and reducing blood flow and breathing. Plus, it can worsen chronic pain, so if you are experiencing prolonged tension and body aches, smoking won't help.

4. **Reduce triggers of stress.**

Unfortunately, there are many situations that we face in life that are totally unavoidable, and quite often, there are more demands than hours in the day to address. It is, therefore, important to seek help with time management and address the more important issues in order of priority. In planning, it is important to allocate time for yourself and pace yourself in achieving your goals.

5. **Proper sleep.**

The average amount of sleep recommended is about eight hours from age fourteen upwards, and it is very important for the normal functioning of the body.

WHAT ARE THE BENEFITS OF SLEEP?

- Sleep is essential for longevity, proper health, and well-being.
- It is important for the restoration and repair of the body.
- It improves your immune system.
- It improves your mental function by improving memory, concentration and problem-solving abilities by forming new neural connections.
- It is important for a healthy heart. Sleep lowers blood pressure and heart rate, so it actually rests the vascular system.
- It reduces stress.
- It regulates blood sugar through hormonal activity during sleep.
- It helps to maintain a healthy weight.

SLEEPING TIPS

- Reduce exposure to electronic devices before sleep. It has been shown that these devices cause brain excitability and, therefore, interfere with sleep.
- Create a quiet, comfortable environment.
- Avoid caffeine before sleep, which sometimes acts as a stimulant that will interfere with sleep.
- Try to be consistent in sleep and wake times for better sleep. Variability in these times tends to reduce the quality of sleep.
- Avoid exercise close to sleep time as endorphins tend to be released during exercise, which can affect the ability to sleep.

6. **Examine your values and live by them.**

The more your actions reflect your beliefs, the better you will feel, no matter how busy your life is. Use your values when choosing your activities.

7. Assert yourself.

It is okay to say "no" to demands on your time and energy that will place too much stress on you. You don't always have to meet the expectations of others.

8. Set realistic goals and expectations.

It is very important not to set unrealistic goals in life. It is impossible to dedicate 100% to every activity simultaneously, so, as mentioned before, being able to prioritize your goals is essential and healthy.
One must be very clear in understanding and accepting that there are things we will never be able to control. Therefore, a stroke is a serious and potentially devastating disease that has ravaged many lives. There are changes that can be made in our lifestyle that can positively impact our general health and the development of this condition. We can start now and choose to take control of our health and destiny.

Those who have had a stroke can reduce the likelihood of a recurrence and improve their current state through rehabilitative care and making intentional decisions to change negative patterns.

Lisa Hoad BSc.
Chemistry & Biochemistry, MBBS
Medical Doctor and Deaconess

LESSONS LEARNED

- The importance of community.

  Two people are better off than one, for they can help each other succeed. If one person falls, the other can reach out and help. But someone who falls alone is in real trouble. Likewise, two people lying close together can keep each other warm. But how can one be warm alone? A person standing alone can be attacked and defeated, but two can stand back-to-back and conquer. Three are even better, for a triple-braided cord is not easily broken. (Ecclesiastes 4:9-12 - NLT).

  Isolation and aloneness at times can be detrimental especially when one needs help or support. It is important to be a part of and not apart from the believing community in fellowship.

- There are always people willing to support rather than condemn you.

- There are far more people rallying for than despising you.

- Always allow the family to break the news of any crisis first.

- Be very sensitive, and not inundate the bereaved or suffering with constant calls at odd hours.

- Be careful about the information posted or spread verbally without checking the source or receiving approval.

- Patiently pray and garner prayerful support on behalf of the hurting.

OTHER BOOKS BY THE AUTHOR

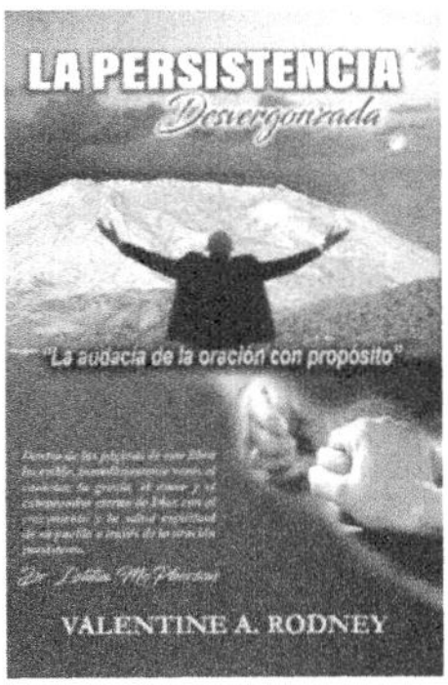

Made in the USA
Middletown, DE
09 September 2024

60091334R00119